Heathen
Warrior

An exploration into the Warrior Ethos within the Northern Tradition

Stuart R Brogan

Published by:

Midgard Books

Glastonbury

England

www.midgardbooks.co.uk

Acknowledgements

First and foremost I would like to thank you, the reader, for purchasing this book. Without you I wouldn't be doing what I am doing.

I raise my mead horn to the following:

My fellow Heathen Warriors Richard Thackway, Tim Bryant, Peter Rowland and Steve Palmer, who helped, advised and spent many hours exploring the outer realms with me. They are truly some of the finest friends a man could have. To my mother, father and brother for their love, support and encouragement in all my endeavours. To all those who have contributed, advised and helped in any way, I thank you. To all those of adventurous spirit wishing to explore, push boundaries and strive to be better, I salute you.

I raise a toast to the ancestors who paved the way through turbulent times and still held strong to their beliefs and way of life. To the High Ones, whom I stand before on my own two feet as a free man:

Hail to you!

To my wife Fiona, the greatest shield maiden a man could have, this is for you.

I love you.

Table of Contents

Heathen Warrior

An Exploration into the Warrior Ethos within the Northern Tradition

by Stuart R Brogan

Chapter One

Introduction to the Heathens

From the misty and windswept North Sea a boat appears unlike any previously seen, a dragon's head at the bow and carrying a dishevelled and brutal horde of savages sent from Hell itself. Shields line the side of their vessel and the sign of the sun wheel is emblazoned upon their sail. Their sole intent: to set ablaze God's holy buildings, defile the woman and kill any who stand in their way. Pillaging and thievery is mandatory and slavery awaits the weak. You may pray, but to no avail. They know not of our Lord; you can't reason with them, for they are void of Christian values. As they make landfall you can hear them scream and shout to their Pagan gods, raven battle standards aloft to the wind, steel drawn and at the ready to put their godless will to the flesh of Christian men, women and *children. You just have enough time to clasp your hands in prayer and look to the heavens above, pleading to the Christ before they are upon you. "From the fury of the North men deliver us, o Lord." The slash of steel: pain and finally, darkness. The Heathen warriors have arrived.*

Wow! All very dramatic would you not agree? The early Christians certainly had a flair for descriptive narratives. Although these are my own words, one can imagine any Monastic follower furiously scribbling down his thoughts as a future warning to his brethren. They did, however, have a good reason to fear these strangers from across the sea. They had been warned that to the north lay a race of sea-dwelling men who plundered their way across Europe and eventually the world, resisting Christian dominance and enslaving and killing any God-fearing Christian that stood before them. But we must ask ourselves: is this an accurate interpretation of the Vikings, or for that matter any tribe dwelling in the Northern hemisphere at this moment in history who held the same ancestral beliefs? Or is it merely a distorted narrow-minded Christian view based solely due on the fact that these men worshipped another set of Gods and had no inclination in giving up their indigenous beliefs in favour of the ones that come from the East without a fight? And who, according to the Christians, had absolutely no moral code - only a lust for battle and blood.

In a time when Christianity was sweeping the globe, forcing its doctrines upon indigenous peoples in an effort to unify the world under Christendom, many tribes and regionally-specific peoples reacted harshly and with hostility to what they perceived as a threat upon their own belief systems and kinfolk: an alien religion and inconceivable threat, thrust upon their world without consent nor wish. The word Heathen simply means someone who is uncivilized, uncultured and who is unconverted to God or any other recognised religion. However, to our Teutonic ancestors, including the Vikings and the native Anglo-Saxons, amongst others, our indigenous faith *was* a recognized religion and belief system long before Christianity spread to the northern shores. Imagine if today a foreign religion tried to assert its dominance in our lands. How do you think the current government would react? This is the dilemma that our ancestors faced all those years ago. Of course, there were other reasons for the Vikings to spread out across the globe, but that is best left for the history books and I am no historian. I am concerned with the subject at hand: the religious and spiritual beliefs of the Heathens and the relationship it has with the warrior within us. As you will see, I stand tall and state to the world that I am a Heathen Warrior and proud to be a member of our ancestral religion regardless of what the doomsayers spout. I am neither ashamed nor embarrassed by my faith and will defend it merits and customs to my last breath.

I think it is safe to assume that you, the reader, has an interest in the indigenous belief system of our ancestors, are seeking information regarding such or are just curious regarding the warrior aspect and how it can relate to you in today's technological and fast paced world. I am of the belief that you are sitting there thinking to yourself, how can a horde of mindless barbarians bring wisdom, creativity and spiritual guidance to me and mine? Can an ancient "Heathen" religion really give us answers to the problems that we all face in an age where so much pressure is placed upon us to have the latest gadgets, the newest car and the biggest house; where all sense of morals has been eradicated and where money is the new God? Can it really have any bearing on the daily grind that most of us find ourselves in whether working nine to five in a corporate office or as a minimum wage cleaner? Can you really be a warrior and walk the warrior path in today's hectic and politically correct world? Some of you may have prior knowledge of the Heathen religion but do you really know anything about the warrior aspect and the role it plays in the spiritual context? As you will see in the following chapters, I shall try and pass on to you the knowledge I have gained through life's rich tapestry of ups and downs. I have to be clear with my intent regarding this book. My intent is not to convert you, nor shall I be turning up on your doorstep and thrusting literature in your hands! I will, however, be sharing some thoughts and personal experiences regarding the warrior in us all and how it keeps us in good stead when faced with life's challenges. We first have to realise that not all battles the warrior faces are physical, but the way we approach them with our spiritual and ethical mindset is universal whether you follow the warrior path or not. The similarities that we share with our distant kin are remarkable and as we will discover, they had the same fears and concerns as we do today. In a world where there are so many belief systems available to us both off the shelf and bespoke, I am of the opinion that we need this folk religion now more than ever before. As a people we need to take a step back and re-connect with our ancestral spirituality. We need to take time to look around us and act appropriately in an objective and honourable way as to make our ancestors proud and to give our children the moral guidance and foundations they need for the future. Great wisdom is available to us if only we would stand up and take notice and listen with open hearts.

I don't profess to be an expert. I certainly don't have all the answers to all the questions you may have, but what I do have is the unshakable belief that the Gods are looking down on their folk and are watching us in our daily lives. When all is said and done, all any of us can do is our very best and whilst striving to become better than we currently are, hope the Gods smile upon our family and folk and bless us with a warm hearth and full bellies. I daresay your curiosity may be panged already and that's great but I must warn you, the path of the Heathen Warrior is not an easy one and don't expect a quick-fix solution to your spiritual problems. It takes a lot of hard work and self-discipline to obtain the knowledge our ancestors possessed, but that's the point of learning. Nothing of worth comes easy or without a price to pay. However hard this road, it is meant to be enjoyable and enrich your everyday life, not become a burden to the point that you lose interest and turn your attentions to something else. I am a firm believer that any culture with such a rich and diverse history such as ours and that does not look to the past for inspiration and clarity is doomed to make the same mistakes in the future. I have a funny feeling you would agree.

When we investigate our ancestral past, we can't help but come up against a barrage of twisted ideologies, misconceptions and out and out lies. We must always try to remain pragmatic in our search for the truth and must resist the temptation to take everything at face value. If we don't, we run the risk of arming ourselves completely with the wrong information, thus weakening our case when talking and promoting our faith. With this in mind, you will see that a reoccurring theme throughout this book is the aspect of personal responsibility. I encourage you to investigate and explore yourself at any given opportunity for I am not here to insist that I am correct in all my musings, but rather give you the starting blocks to formulate your own journey of spiritual discovery. I'm sure that when you mention the word "Heathen" people's reactions will vary depending on their understanding of the word itself or the place it holds within a historical context. Don't be discouraged. As with everything, it takes time. Each person will start their own spiritual journey at different times and this usually happens when he or she least expects it.

Talking of which, are you ready to get started? You are? Good. Sit back, relax, maybe make yourself a drink, hail the Gods on high and get ready to break out the fine china. The Heathen Warrior is coming to dinner.

Chapter Two

The Warrior, The Hero

"A wayfarer should not walk unarmed,

But have his weapons to hand:

He knows not when he may need a spear,

Or what menace meet on the road."

The Havamal

Throughout the ages and since time began, the warrior has always been vencrated and placed upon a pedestal of honour and virtue in almost every culture across the globe. He was held in high regard and used to protect their people in times of war and as a symbol that the young could aspire to, a symbol of Honour, Strength and Fortitude, a shining beacon of hope in darker times. From the vast plains of Mongolia to the rugged mountains of Norway, from the arid deserts of Africa to the mist shrouded Fens of Britain, the warrior ethos is ever present. It is even depicted in ancient cave paintings across the globe, drawn hundreds of years before "religion" and yet so little is known or for that matter, explored, with relation to any semblance of spirituality. As a culture we seem to be brainwashed into believing that a warrior is just that and that alone, unable to make any rational decision, a slave to the whims of his/her superior , totally void of emotion and a spiritual vacuum. However, when we start to sift our way through history we began to realise that spirituality has always played a major role in a warrior's ethos; indeed it was crucial to his/her development regardless of what religious path he/she follows. One only has to look for example at the Knights of Europe during the middle ages, crusading across the world to rid the "Holy land" of the Islamic threat, using their martial prowess to absolve themselves of sin and to win back God's favour. Christian scholars talk amongst themselves and praise the Knights Templar for their selfless work and piety and praise their name for being good "religious" men. However, history has shown us that they were also brutal and without remorse and could be capable of immense cruelty, all in the name of "God". By pure definition, their acts as warriors during war was all in the name of religion. So how can one be devoid of it? (I must point out without prejudice that all religions have had times chronicled that would appear detrimental to their teachings). I am of the opinion that all warriors need some sort of faith or moralistic code to justify their actions, without which they are nothing but a mindless thug.

With this in mind could we not surmise that our views on the Vikings, Anglo-Saxons and other Heathen peoples are a little distorted? I'm not for one moment suggesting that our ancestors did not commit horrendous acts of cruelty, are completely blameless and that they spent all their time weaving and cuddling small furry animals, and that all the history books are in fact wrong. What I am saying is that history is exactly that, his-story, one person's view influenced by his/hers own beliefs and opinions, because after all, history is written by the victor. How many eyewitness accounts actually exist regarding the Heathens? Most are written by the very enemies of Heathen culture, hence the one-sided bad press. A single person's view gets written down and that becomes fact because the "villains" are not there to defend or counteract the supposed event. Over time, the more people who read the statement tell others, who in turn write accounts whilst adding their own imaginative flair; none of whom were even there and I doubt have any real knowledge at all. All of a sudden there are thousands of accounts of the same event, each one with slightly different elements depending on the author's literary ability, sense of imagination, personal moral code and spiritual beliefs.

But there is hope! Despite the warrior's bad press over the years, people seem to be waking up and taking a renewed interest in re-kindling and re-discovering the knowledge and spirituality our ancestors possessed. Across the world, living history enthusiasts recreate day to day living and battles at festivals and special historic events, having fun with family and kin whilst educating the public at large with a tangible link to our ancestors. Authors write fantastical novels of a lost golden heroic age, stirring our imagination and giving us a welcome break from today's hectic world. Film makers weave their craft creating visually majestic films using modern science and special effects to transport us back to a bygone era. Watching these movies as a young boy held me captivated and enthralled me to explore and research everything I could regarding the strong and unflinching warrior ethos, to strive to be a better person. As a modern day Heathen Warrior I, like so many others, had an interest in martial arts and the warrior culture from the East, influenced by the media around me at the time. However, it wasn't until I was older that I realised that my own culture was filled with heroic battles, honourable warriors and a set of values that in my opinion surpassed that of our eastern neighbours. Over the years I read as much as I could and was amazed at the wealth of knowledge that lay hidden amongst the annals of historical documents and the myths and legends from all across the Northern hemisphere. The more I explored the more I found that our ancestral warriors had a complete way of life that extended throughout family and kin. These warriors were also artists, musicians, storytellers, fathers, sons and husbands and yet they were labelled barbarians and vermin by the Christian faith and other so called "civilized" societies. A strong social structure bound all in the tribe together, a shared sense of equality creating a stable and unified people, a human trait I believe we have lost in today's densely populated world.

But there is hope! In the 21st century the symbolism of the warrior seems to be creeping back into our lives and is becoming more socially acceptable. It has managed to claw its way back into modern culture thanks to movies like *The Lord of The Rings* trilogy, which I have to say is the perfect paragon and poster campaign for the Heathen Warrior. A group of likeminded kin flung together to defeat an evil force, it is a tale of honour, courage, friendship, loyalty, love and trust. What is a better influence for today's misguided youth, its kings and leaders honourable, its subjects willing to defend and lay down their lives for kin? (In the next chapter I shall expand on the nine noble virtues, a set of values we as Heathens adhere to and believe in whole-heartedly.) Who in their right mind cannot be touched by the message of hope presented in such a film, a tale of great valour in a time when darkness seems to be all around us?

With all these new movies comes the subsequent and inevitable product machine. Hence, modern media moguls have realised that in today's modern world the heroic ideal sells products. Everyone has the deep-seeded desire to be the "hero" in some way or another, to vanquish the school bully perhaps or to put other people's safety before their own, but feel trapped by today's "must have" consumerism and the "put yourself first" mentality. I can honestly say (and am not ashamed to admit), that I myself have felt these same feelings at certain points in my life. Situations have presented themselves with dilemmas, which armed with the knowledge I now have, I would have handled in a different way. I acted in either fear or naivety but deep down knew at the time I was acting against my moral code; even so, and to my shame, I acted without honour. So can we really blame ourselves for buying into the corporate sales pitch? How many times have you seen an advert for a large four wheel drive vehicle alone in the vast wilderness with the voiceover informing you that you can be a rugged hero, or that the new special fragrance advertised is for "real" men of the world, crafted with a shot of a rather handsome stubbly beefcake of a man, making you puff your chest out and thus agreeing with the marketing campaign for fear of feeling less of a man? The above examples may seem extreme to you but when you stop and have a really hard think about what you see and hear in just one 24-hour period of your weekly routine you will be amazed how much we are bombarded with the hero persona. Whether it's to tempt us into parting with our hard earned cash for the latest must-have gadget or to lure us to the nearest multiplex to enjoy

Hollywood's newest blockbuster, the sales pitch is always the same. With the kind of money thrown at such campaigns and our own personal desire to be "more" than we already are, it would seem that the big corporations are on to a good thing. As with the silver screen and the invention of the home television set in the modern world being a focal point for family learning and gathering, our ancestors also had their own ways of entertaining, educating and enlightening the family and kin. It may surprise you that storytelling and the spoken word was of upmost importance to the Heathen tribes, in fact to be a bard or skald was considered an honourable and noble vocation amongst the people of the so-called "dark ages". In a time when hardly any Heathen peoples used any semblance of the written word, all tales of heroic prowess were passed on in an oral way from father to child. Many of the tales told from what we today call the Eddas or the Sagas contained adventurers of both the Gods and mortal men alike. Of course they have been written down now, but when reading them we can envisage in our mind's eye our ancestors gathering around a camp fire whilst listening intently as the Skald recounts the adventures of Beowulf or about when Ragnarok rages and the Gods do battle with the frost giants. If you have not read them, may I suggest you purchase them as they make for fantastic reading and give an insight into Heathen life and a glimpse of the skill in which our ancestors were able to weave their oral magic. I shall, however, be referring to such tales in later chapters in an attempt to link our ancestors' beliefs with our faith today. As with much of today's literature, the actual stories seem to be specific to the social and political climate of the time. Usually the villain of the piece would have done some kind of wrongdoing and of course the "hero" or "warrior" would strive to bring him to justice. You would be forgiven in thinking that it sounded like a generic modern story, but you would be wrong. Nearly all the characters have human flaws as well as strengths and weaknesses and hardly any character, including the protagonist or antagonist, were without some sort of personal turmoil or inner dilemma. In other words, by giving ALL the characters some sort of emotional problem the storyteller superimposed very real and relevant social questions at that moment in time, questions relative to the immediate kin. Of course the effect of such a rich skaldic skill was to create empathy between the heroic characters and the audience. The normal working class Heathens listening to this would of undoubtedly thought, "It's good to know that warriors, heroes and even the Gods themselves face the same trials and tribulations as I", thus forging a spiritual and moral bond between kin, family, faith and the world around them. However, to confuse empathy and kindness for weakness would be a mistake.

As Heathen Warriors, we must always maintain a pragmatic and realistic view of the world around us. Like our ancestors, we would love to live in a world where war is a thing of the past and our families were safe from senseless violence committed by savage and non-moralistic men. However, to think we actually live in such a world is at best naive and at worst criminal. I myself have travelled extensively and have seen the many wonders the world has to offer but I have also seen the very worst of human nature. Thus it is always the smartest idea to hope for the best, but plan for the worst.

It is my belief that the warrior aspect lives within us all. We all have the desire and if pushed to it, have the capability to defend our loved ones from any threat and to keep them from harm's way. I don't think there is anyone that would let something horrific happen to a loved one if they could intervene and stop it. Therefore, wouldn't you agree that the selfless act and risking of your life for another puts us in the remit of "The Hero"? Of course there are those in society that have jobs that entail them risking their lives on behalf of the rest of us every day, such as soldiers who risk their lives defending us from tyranny, the firemen who save us from a burning building and the policemen whose job it is to keep civilians safe from the predators in our society. All these people are held in high regard because we give them the powers and the skill to enter dangerous situations, safe in the knowledge that we trust them, even putting our lives into their hands. I would say these brave men and women are no different from our ancestors. The warrior ethos is the same, only society has changed and with such a fast-paced world our mindset should also try to keep up. These are the kind of people that should be energising our children and inspiring them to become the best person they can be, but if we see a "bad apple" within these honourable vocations do we discard and tarnish them as a whole? No, we don't. So why do we as a whole look badly upon our Heathen ancestors and believe them all to be barbaric and so radically different from us today?

So let's cut to the chase, shall we? In my opinion when you really break it down to its purist form, the Warrior Aspect is the decision made by the individual to place themselves in harm's way in order to protect his family, kin, faith or anything else he/she truly believes in, regardless of the risk or at least knowing the risks, but accepting it regardless of the possible detrimental outcomes. Now to me that really does sound like something we should all aspire to and have the courage to explore, but to be reckless and to use this newfound inner strength and clarity of purpose without some kind of temperance and restraint can be dangerous. We need to keep ourselves grounded, to know when to use our abilities and to evaluate whether we are using them for the right reasons. It all seems like common sense, doesn't it? You may even be thinking that I am teaching you how to suck eggs, but how can we be totally sure we are acting with the best intentions or rather, doing it to inflate or satisfy our own ego? Hence the introductions of spirituality into the Warriors' world view. This leads us seamlessly on to the Moral Compass and the Nine Noble Virtues.

Chapter Three

The Nine Noble Virtues and the Moral Compass

"A man should be loyal through life to friends,

And return gift for gift,

Laugh when they laugh,

but with lies repay

A false foe who lies."

The Havamal

In this chapter I shall explore what most modern Heathens regard as the foundations of our faith, how it affects our daily lives and how we interact with those around us.

To start with I feel it is important to inform you that the Northern Tradition is what's known as a "reconstructionist" religion, meaning there isn't a vast amount of written information regarding the rituals and rites of our ancestors. We are only able to sift through second hand accounts, poems, Eddas and other historical accounts, then fill in the blanks as best we can based on an educated guess. Please remember that varying opinions abound and mine may court controversy as I draw some conclusions that may seem a little "farfetched". However, I state they are plausible and to my mind, probable when we look at the wider picture.

Within our tradition there is a set of verse known as *The Havamal,* also known as the sayings of the High One; in other words, they are Odin's tips to us mortals for living a productive and worthwhile life. Most Heathens use the term "Sacred Text" when discussing *The Havamal* and in one way I would agree that within our belief system it is the nearest thing to having a "religious book". However, we must always be cautious when reading and interoperating the High One's words for as we know it is easy to misconstrue the meaning of such holy publications and the ideas presented are open to interpretation, depending on the person reading and assessing the information. Personally I look at it as a guide book to help and to assist us and should always be viewed within the context of the modern age we live in. That being said, the "message" behind the teachings is resolute and of profound importance.

Our ancestors believed that these Nine Noble Virtues were the core elements for a decent, hardworking and honourable member of their society. They themselves did not use the Nine Noble Virtues as they are seen today. They didn't use a specific word but rather a descriptive dialog to describe each virtue in the context of a story or a poem and the everyday actions of the folk. (With many different languages and dialects spoken throughout the Northern Hemisphere and amongst the different Heathen tribes, stories describing the virtue were easier to understand.) It is only in later years (the 1970s to be precise) that modern Heathens decided to utilise a single word to emphasise each virtue. It must be said that there are dividing opinions regarding the Nine Noble Virtues. Some modern Heathens do not subscribe to the virtues and state that they are a modern invention with no basis in Heathen lore; however, I believe they are important as they act as a short reminder of admirable qualities within our faith. Of course opinions vary and are subjective.

There are many terms and titles for our faith, Northern Tradition, Asatru, Odinisim, Wodenisim and Heathenism to name but a few. Some are regional-specific like English Anglo-Saxon or Norse Viking Heathenism. These are more likely to have different ideas regarding the ritual side of the faith due to geographical location but it is generally accepted that the Virtues or the reasoning behind them are of paramount importance regardless of where you are located and what "strand" of Heathenism you practice, even though we may call our faith by a different name. I think we are all singing from the same hymn sheet, excuse the pun! But let's get back to the task at hand shall we?

Some of the issues raised will seem like common sense, others will make you think and evaluate your own actions in this crazy modern world of ours. Others may force you to really take stock and ask some deep and potentially illuminating questions regarding what you would do in a similar situation. The core reasoning of the virtues are of immense importance to all Heathens and we strive to attain them in our daily lives. I shall list them with a description of how they are utilised within the Heathen Warrior ethos and will even throw in a brief personal experience if I think appertains or re-enforces the message. Some will be of a humorous nature while others will be more serious but all will be truthful and honest. I shall also refer to *The Havamal* and use quotes that show a direct link from the ancestors' belief system to the virtue itself and how it appertains to us in the modern age. I could write an entire book regarding the Virtues within the Northern Tradition as a whole. However, as I have stated before, I want to try and be Warrior specific, so please forgive me if I digress. Let's start with something different, something that I feel is crucial to the spiritual and emotional development of the Heathen Warrior. It is the base component that determines our actions and reactions to conflict or other choices we face; something I call The Moral Compass.

The Moral Compass

"Moderate at council should a man be,

Not brutal and over bearing:

Among the bold the bully will find

Others as bold as he"

The Havamal

At what age do you think we can ascertain right from wrong without the external influence of others? Do you believe that we can only make decisions based on our own experiences, or from what we remember our parents instilling in us when we were young children? You might have thought about these questions at some point in your life but can you honestly answer them in a full and comprehensive way or is your conscious mind unable to choose a specific time or age when you realised right from wrong? It may seem strange to pose such questions in anything other than a psychology reference book but these are some of the questions we as Heathen Warriors must ask ourselves.

Morality is a major factor in our faith. Its driving force and influence in our decision-making cannot be underestimated and must be taught and explored from an early age, then reinforced through a close-knit community, involving everyone within the tribe. Social interaction and spiritual teachings must be of high priority within the Warrior training as well as the martial training. In our faith everyone has the right to express an opinion regardless of social standing, thus making everyone equal when sat at the same table. Equality is also a major issue to the Heathen Warrior in all aspects of his education. Morality and equality go hand in hand and need to be nurtured and given the opportunity to grow.

As we travel the Warrior path we must embrace the fact that we do not have any right to force our views or faith upon anyone else. We are steadfast in the belief that our kin should not venture out into unknown territory and "convert" other peoples to our way of thinking; to do so would be a complete contradiction of our faith. The majority of us believe that the individual finds the faith and not the other way around. I myself felt a sense of "coming home" when I found my faith all those years ago. However I had always tried to live my life in accordance with the Heathen Warrior ethos but never really knew it had a name. Personal choice and the freedom to make that choice without fear of retaliation is a right gifted to all from the Gods. A link to your own indigenous religious system is a right all folk should have regardless of what faith they practice. I have no right to force my way of life onto anyone else and likewise I don't expect others to force their views upon me and mine. A mutual respect should exist between different tribes; if everyone can rely on the honourable nature of the next community and everyone has been taught from an early age a status quo of sorts is produced, thus avoiding conflict. However, history has shown us that religion is often used by the powerful to subjugate indigenous peoples for the purpose of resources, forging alliances or simply to attain more power.

Many Monotheistic religions look down upon our faith with disdain and ridicule for they have the mistakenly belief we lack a moral code to which to live by due to the fact we don't have a set of "things" we must abstain from, but rather a set of "things" we should aspire to. We are adamant in the fact that we do not fall to our knees begging the Gods on high to forgive our mistakes; rather we stand before them as proud, free men and women stating, "I have made a mistake but I have learned from it, thank you for the learning opportunity!" I also want to point out that because we are a Polytheistic religion we have many Gods and Goddesses each with different characteristics, temperaments and motivations. Just because one God disapproves of your actions, that's not to say another wouldn't be overjoyed. Each God or Goddess is as different as you and me; sometimes they listen and respond, sometimes they won't simply because they are in a bad mood! The Heathen Warrior believes that to punish oneself or to deny ourselves the luxuries or simple pleasures that are afforded to us here in this realm of Midgard to be a pointless waste of time and energy. The Gods want us and expect us to stand up, experience and grow into the best person we can. We cannot do this without making mistakes or by being denied the choice to make a wrong decision due to religious piety. Our moral compass cannot evolve and take shape if we are fully aware that after all is said and done and the repercussions of our actions are felt, our Gods can just forgive us regardless of what we have done. This takes away any sense of personal responsibility, thus keeping us in a state of self-imposed religious compliance.

The Virtues

HONESTY

It may seem an easy one for us to comprehend and to adhere to but yet many of us are guilty at some stage in our lives for not sticking to the truth, or being economical with our true intentions. In war, sometimes it is practical to use stealth and misdirection to our advantage when dealing with a formidable opponent, for example. In our daily lives we may lie because we believe that our deceptions are justified be it for fear of reprisals or an outcome not to our liking. That's not to say we are bad people and are not worthy to remain a Heathen Warrior, for as we discussed earlier, we have to make mistakes in order for our moral compass to find "true north".

As we grow as Warriors our main adversary is fear, fear of any conflict thrust upon us, be it physical or otherwise. There is a vast difference between confidence in our own abilities and arrogance. T the wise Warrior knows his own as well as his enemies' strengths and weaknesses, thus giving him the upper hand. The main issue is that we be honest with ourselves and the reasons that motivate our actions. Are we fighting for ego and pride or is there a more moralistic and admirable reason urging us into action? Only you can answer that and the only time you can ask that question is at the "void" state, that split second before a confrontation. But be aware, to ask such a question of yourself may lead you to a conclusion you would rather not know. If we are truly honest with ourselves regarding our reasons before reacting to a situation we can take solace in the fact after the event that we can feel truly justified in our response.

"An ill-tempered, unhappy man

Ridicules all he hears,

Makes fun of others, refusing always

To see the faults in himself"

The Havamal

Personal example:

A few years ago I was working as a nightclub doorman in a different town from where I lived. One night a huge monster of a man approached the door, drunk and extremely aggressive in his demeanour. Because I was new to this particular club, I was unaware of who this man was and of his violent reputation. (I later found out that he made a habit of spending his weekends travelling around, putting doorman into the hospital just for kicks!)

My years of experience as a doorman kicked in and I realised that this man should not be allowed into the club and was quite clearly out for trouble. He tried to push past me and into the club. I placed my hand on his chest and gently pushed him back, informing him that he wasn't allowed in due to his drunkenness, and that he should go home. For the next five minutes the man threw insult after insult at me whilst turning redder and redder. I was sure an attack was imminent. Then, as if on cue, the man threw all his body weight into a right punch straight towards my face. Now let's stop there, shall we? At this point I entered the fight or flight stage, a chemical and psychological response to a dangerous and life-threatening situation. Time seemed to slow down; at this point I was in the "void", a split-second to choose my reaction. Should I hit the man before he hits me? Should I run away? Should I wait until he hits me, then hit him? Or should I move, then try to reason with him? Some of you may think you know how you would react, but ask yourself honestly. Until you are in that situation none of us truly know.

Bang! I side stepped to the right and hit him with a right punch, knocking him to the floor. After a few seconds he got up and walked away without a word. Now the point of the story is not to boast about the confrontation, but to highlight the fact that I was honest with myself and had assessed the situation. I truly believed this man was a threat and had to be dealt with accordingly. Afterwards, I felt that I had engaged the man, not because of my ego but because I was morally justified to protect myself from a violent force that wouldn't respond to conversation and only respected strength. If he had not thrown a punch I would not have had any justification other than ego to fight this man.

COURAGE

I absolutely believe that it takes true courage to live by and adhere to the Nine Noble Virtues in today's every changing and materialistic world. In an age where there are so many distractions fighting for our attention and so many negative forces at work willing us to lie down and give up, courage is our greatest weapon. The word "courage" may conjure up an image of a warrior standing alone upon a battlefield facing insurmountable odds. However I feel in today's world it is more akin to facing life's everyday challenges that seem to bombard us all - raising a family, paying the bills, etc. Any problem, dilemma or choice faced, no matter how small, affects different people in a completely different way. What some may overcome with ease may be crippling for another. Phobias are an obvious choice to use. I myself am scared of heights and needles, yet you may have no problem with them. I need courage to face my own personal fear, yet for you it is of no consequence.

How many times in life have you been put down or made to feel that you can never attain your dreams - you are just an underling and your boss is the creator of the universe! - but yet you have had the courage to go for it anyway? To stand tall and declare, "I want this and I'm going to give it my best shot regardless!" - now that's true courage. It is, however, obvious that not all of us will be successful or climb the lofty heights of stardom, BUT at least we have had the courage to give it ago. I would rather try and fail than to say, "What if"!

"The coward believes he will live forever

If he holds back in the battle,

But in old age he shall have no peace

Though spears have spared his limbs"

The Havamal

Personal Example:

I am Diabetic. For years I controlled it with tablets and diet; but if I'm honest I wasn't doing a good enough job (much to my wife's annoyance). Sometime ago I was basically told that if I didn't start taking insulin by injection I could very well end up in hospital with a kidney transplant. Now, I have to say again that I am terrified of needles, so much so I swore to my wife that I would rather die than spend the rest of my life injecting myself. My wife stood by me and was a tower of support even though I was a shivering wreck!

The day came when I had my meeting at the hospital with the specialist nurse and had to face the stark reality that I had to make a choice. I summoned up all the courage I could muster and faced my fear. I now inject insulin four times a day, and have been for over a year now. I don't enjoy it, but I had the courage to do it anyway.

So let's be blunt now. If your moral compass tells you that something is right and that you must defend your actions or reasonings, then have the courage of your convictions and stand true to your beliefs. It does not matter how big or small the battle is or whether you win or lose; it's about having the courage to face it head-on and doing what feels right, even in the face of adversity.

HONOUR

This one is probably the trickiest to convey. Each of us, by way of our moral compass can define what honour means to us as individuals. I feel that our own sense of honour determines our actions regarding others and how we interact with them. If we are wronged do we retaliate, and if so were we justified? Our outwardly projection to those around us also determine if we are honourable. How are we regarded within our own tribe or amongst our work colleagues? Would our kinsmen stand tall and say "Yes, he is an honourable man?" We must also be aware that our honour or lack of affects our children and may cast a shadow over them once we pass on if our kinsmen deem our actions not to be of an honourable nature. Our actions in life denote what kind of standing we have in the next realm and whether the Gods look favourably at us. This has nothing to do with social status in terms of wealth or power but rather by deeds and actions.

I am of the opinion that honour is all the other virtues rolled into one, the main virtue to which we should live by; your moral compass, personal passion and wisdom denotes and installs in you the very essence of honour. It is the final result from the nurturing of all other skills and training. It is the final cake cooked from all the different and individual ingredients.

"The fool who fancies he is full of wisdom

While he sits by his hearth at home.

Quickly finds when questioned by others

That he knows nothing at all"

The Havamal

Personal Example:

A long time ago I was walking home and spotted a wallet discarded in the grass. I stopped and opened it up. To my surprise there was about thirty pounds in cash and lots of credit cards. I looked at the driver's license and recognised the person to be a local shop keeper just around the corner. Even though I was hard up at the time and was out of work and didn't really like the shop keeper (a horrible vindictive man), I decided to return the wallet to him anyway and did just that. However, I didn't even get a thank you! He just snatched the wallet, checked the money and returned to what he was doing. Now as you can guess, I was pretty annoyed at this. I had gone out of my way to help someone I didn't even regard as kin and yet received no gratification. As I walked away I knew in my heart of hearts that I had done the right thing. It was only a week later that I won some money! Maybe the Gods thought I should get a bonus for doing the right thing!

LOYALTY

As a Heathen Warrior we are bound by loyalty to protect, defend and be true to our family, kin and faith. Our ancestors believed that within the warrior aspect any wrongdoing or act of violence upon a kinsman had to be avenged or a heavy fine placed upon the attacker. This may seem harsh by today's socially acceptable rules but it would not only act as a sign of strength but an immediate response would stop any chance of a blood feud developing between tribes, thus keeping war to a minimum. It was a practical approach to law and order as well as safe guarding the integrity and honour of the tribe. Of course such a compromise would also ensure that future generations would have heroic stories to tell and sing about, thus creating and immortalising the tribe in the future, a solution that served many purposes.

Our ancestors used the terms Troth meaning an unshakable and binding bond to others and Orlog meaning fate, destiny or doom. Troth and Orlog are an intertwining concept with that of loyalty (I will elaborate on these in a later chapter). In today's materialistic world, loyalty is a rare virtue. In an era when we are all facing hard times both socially and economically, taking the "easy" way out and turning on the people around us shouldn't even be an option; however, some deem themselves justified because in their eyes it is a dog-eat-dog world. To a certain degree I agree with the fact that you have to look out for yourself but certainly not at the expense of family and kin. If you are, however, wronged by a disloyal person you are completely justified to return the favour. To be loyal we need to be honest with ourselves and have the courage to do what is right and for the best for our faith, folk and family. It is the essence of our faith in regards to future generations and our image portrayed to the outside world. It may require that you sacrifice something or forgo your true wishes for the good of the tribe, a sacrifice for the greater good.

A Heathen Warrior on the battlefield had to have loyalty to his kin and the courage to fight, thus creating an honourable member of society worthy of song and spoken word. If, however, a warrior fled from the field of battle, he would be shunned by society. The shame would not only be placed upon him but on that of his children until a son did a deed worthy of honour, thus erasing the relative's disgrace. To remain loyal to our faith, kin and family is without question needed and expected regardless of how big the battle faced.

"Fire is needed by the newcomer

Whose knees are frozen numb;

Meat and clean linen a man needs

Who has fared across the fells,"

The Havamal

Personal example:

Not too long ago a new rule was implemented that stated no jewellery of any kind was to be worn in the warehouse where I worked as a forklift driver. This included rings, watches and necklaces. I wear a Thor's Hammer necklace, and as a sign of my loyalty to my faith, never take it off. Now, as it was a food manufacturing plant I would agree that if I was in the production hall where they packaged raw goods I would have agreed to my boss' wishes; however I was nowhere near the packaging hall so decided that I was well within my rights to fight the decision based on religious grounds. I proceeded to do some research regarding health and safety regulations and freedom of religion legislations, then presented my findings to my personnel department. The result was that I now have special dispensation to wear my necklace at work. To some fellow workers I was a wind-up merchant, to my bosses a troublesome pain in the backside; however, my loyalty to my faith is such that I will stand my ground and have the courage to fight any battle, no matter how it manifests itself!

DISCIPLINE

Having discipline gives us the building blocks and resolve to be the best we can be within our faith and community as well as giving us the opportunity to attain our personal dreams or accomplishing personal goals. We must always strive to be harder on ourselves than anyone else, for us as warriors need to lead by example, to show others within our faith and family that it isn't a case of "do what I say not as I do", thus making them feel we are superior in some way and they are less of a man or woman. We must help and nurture discipline within others and help them to reach a similar standard, be it emotionally, spiritually or with the fighting arts.

I daresay that we have all started things in our lives at one time or another full of enthusiasm and vigour only to lose interest within a few months, such as a new hobby or a job. I know I am guilty of this!

I have to be honest with you, my mind whizzes around at a hundred miles an hour and I have to admit sometimes I lack the discipline needed to complete the project at hand. I go at a new interest hell for leather and full of good intentions but then either lose momentum or interest, thus stopping and moving on to something else. Obviously this is the virtue I have the most trouble with! I told you I wasn't perfect! However, in my defence I must say that when it comes to my faith and family I am resolute in my discipline regarding taking it seriously and being the best father, husband, son and Heathen Warrior I can be.

"Wise is he not who is never silent,

Mouthing meaningless words:

A glib tongue that goes on chattering

Sings to its own harm"

The Havamal

Personal example:

This book! I know, it's a funny example. Before you start laughing, this book has been a labour of love for me. Sometimes it has been frustrating, sometimes laborious and there have been times when I have sat staring at a blank screen unsure of how to put my emotions and ideas into words. No matter how hard the journey I had the discipline to see it through and the courage to stick at a project of which I was unsure how it would be received. All I know is that I was supposed to write it and the

Gods appreciate me giving it my best shot and most importantly, that the learning journey was just as, if not more important than the final destination.

HOSPITALITY

Hospitality is not only one of the virtues but to me a common courtesy afforded to those who visit your home and hearth. Of course you don't just invite anyone into your home without first making some sort of bond or trust. I myself let very few people into my inner sanctum but those who are let in are welcomed with open arms and are instructed to make themselves at home. Our ancestors had kin spread the length and breadth of the country and visits were few and far between due to the distances involved. So if a kinsman took the time and effort to visit, a great responsibility was bestowed upon the household whom was receiving said guest. Of course this does not mean giving away all your worldly possessions but the sharing of food, drink, hearth and shelter. In our faith Odin sometimes takes the guise of a peasant traveller wandering the land, watching and assessing his folk and the last thing a Heathen Warrior needs is to land himself in hot water with the Allfather!

As a Heathen Warrior there will be times when you must be a guest in another's home for training purposes. You may also invite your fellow kinsmen to train at your home. Of course hospitality is crucial when such bonds are developing. In battle you must put your life into the hands of the kinsman next to you and his in yours and he might just well be miffed that you helped yourself to his last biscuit without asking!

Even though I am a strong advocate for the phrase "charity begins at home", I and many Heathens believe that it is our responsibility to help others less fortunate than ourselves whenever possible. We truly believe that it revitalises the soul and brings us inner peace, especially in the modern world. One has to be pragmatic when opening our homes and hearths to others for there are a lot of people of dubious character around who would take advantage of you and give nothing in return. When I invite guests into my home, my wife and I treat them as one of the family but expect our home to be treated with respect. Although I believe help should be offered by the guest, I would not accept it because it was my choice to let the person in. The gesture is, of course, appreciation in itself. The guest would also be expected to offer conversation or news and join in with feasting, not just sit in the corner silently grateful for a hot meal! I know that everyone I invite into my home is aware of my faith and acts accordingly as do I when I am the person visiting another.

"If you find a friend you fully trust

And wish for his good-will,

exchange thoughts,

exchange gifts,

Go often to his house"

The Havamal

Personal example:

A very good friend of mine and fellow Heathen Warrior had moved away but due to circumstances moved back to our home town. He was unemployed and was short of funds but I felt it was my duty as a Heathen and a kinsman to give as much assistance as I could. At this time I also was short of money but invited my friend around and offered food and drink whenever possible. We didn't have a lot and it certainly wasn't huge feasts but I know if the roles were reversed he would do the same for me and my family. He was a gracious guest and never took advantage of my hospitality, thus cementing a firm and strong relationship both in the present and for the future. There are times in all our lives when we have no choice but to accept help from those closest to us. We may not like the fact that we need it and feel less of a Heathen for accepting it, but that's part of the learning process all Heathen Warriors must undertake.

INDUSTRIOUSNESS

As a Heathen Warrior the spiritual, emotional and martial arts skills do not come overnight. We must spend time developing and harnessing our skills to a level we feel appropriate, when all our movements become second nature. I personally feel that I am at the stage where I know enough to help me in tight spots and do not feel the necessity to continue regular training. Repetition of a few moves so it becomes ingrained in muscle memory is in my preferred method of training. Some of my friends, however, still train religiously (excuse the pun) because they love the ritual of training in itself even though they are perfectly capable of handling themselves at any given time. I do like to keep my hand in with some fighting disciplines like boxing. One of my Heathen Warrior friends is a very good and formidable boxer and I personally love to train with him. It's fun and a good workout even though my training partners are much fitter than me! We all have our strengths and weaknesses.

There are three of us in my immediate training circle and we all bring different styles and disciplines to the mix. I myself have studied different martial arts over the years ranging from specialist military close combat styles to traditional Karate. As I have said, one of my friends is a boxer and the other comes from a Muay Thai and kickboxing background. When we get together, we exchange ideas and see what works. We are all of the opinion that "less is more". You don't need to learn a thousand techniques; all you have to do is master four or five. It is mainly your experience that determines how you react. Our ancestors were formidable warriors and I would assume "borrowed" fighting ideas from anyone they fought. If it worked I'm sure they would have amalgamated it into their own fighting techniques.

To strive to better oneself, be a Heathen or other is a human trait that we all share. No matter what community we live in or what faith we practice we all have the deep desire to better ourselves for our own benefit and that of our children and our kin. Of course this does not just mean material wealth and the trappings of modern life but spiritually and emotionally, too. Our ancestors realised that hard work and focus were needed to survive and that things would not be just handed to them on a plate. If we want it, we must work for it. In today's welfare society there are a lot of people who are happy to sit back, do nothing and expect handouts from the rest of us. Of course if you are truly in need it would be against our faith not to help; but if you have the ability to evolve and make changes to your circumstances but choose not to, then you are not worthy to be included in the Heathen collective. The Gods help those who help themselves. You may hate the job you're in and long for something better but feel trapped by the pressures society puts on us. If you desire a change, no matter how small, you can achieve it. It is not only commendable that we stay in jobs we hate to keep a roof over our families head, food in their bellies and clothes on their backs but expected and deemed honourable, noble and deserving of respect from those closest to us.

However, if we focus our belief, sharpen our will and strive for something better we can achieve greatness. Some want wealth while others want social standing and power. I want true happiness for me and mine. My dream would be that I can make a living out of what I love to do, be it art, writing or music, to be able to help and in some small way progress my faith and assist others on a similar path. This does not mean that I want to be super rich and world famous, far from it! I am a private person; as long as I could provide for my family whilst doing something I love I would be humbled and consider that true happiness.

"In the fool who acquires cattle and lands,

Or wins a woman's love,

His wisdom wanes with his waxing pride,

He sinks from sense to conceit."

The Havamal

Personal example:

Some years ago my wife and I moved to the town of Glastonbury, England. After a while of working in dead-end jobs, we decided to open a small shop selling all manner of goods relating to Heathenism and our ancestral beliefs. This was something the town itself had no idea about and at that time had no inclination of selling such products; but we knew that it was a gap in the market and felt sure the Gods were willing us to do it! As any good pagan will tell you, the town of Glastonbury is not only famous for the festival (which isn't actually in Glastonbury but five miles outside it), but is a pilgrimage destination for all those walking the path of any of the earth-based pagan religions. We had our dream of running our own little shop selling quality goods at reasonable prices. We both fell in love with the Somerset town and felt it was where we both belonged. After a little property searching and money wrangling we found a small shop unit and scrambled enough funds together to get us off the ground. We then started to get it ready for a grand opening, excited by the opportunities that lay before us. Once the shop was opened we were amazed by the reaction from locals and customers alike. We went from nothing to having a great reputation within months. People came to our shop purely by word of mouth and from all over the country, and soon our modest little shop was becoming well known overseas. We had regular customers from Germany, Norway, Iceland, Italy and other countries. We were very happy and glad that our hard work was starting to pay off. Originally we sold Celtic and Norse goods but within a few months we realised that the Norse and Heathen goods were what people were really after. We were becoming a specialist shop for the Heathen community. At this time we were the only shop of its kind in the whole of the U.K and soon began to be known locally as "The Viking Shop".

Things were going extremely well apart from the fact that our rent was ridiculously high considering the size of the shop and that our landlord was becoming incredibly erratic and somewhat aggressive towards tenants, thus causing friction which began to create an air of distrust. After two years of mismanagement, threats of violence and the childish behaviour of our so-called landlord we decided to leave the shop and so did some very good friends of ours who were also renting a retail space next door to us. Once we had left we felt like we had lost a limb. Our modest little shop had become a social gathering point for all to have a chat and a cup of tea and to be honest we both felt like we had had our guts ripped out, that we had failed and that all our dreams had been crushed. However, on reflection I have come to realise the true result of our endeavours. Whilst we had been there we had become friends with some of the best and most genuine people I have ever had the privilege to meet, and both my wife and I have forged friendships with some truly amazing folk and feel honoured to call them friends. Our shop was not only well respected but became a permanent fixture within the community that all remember; in fact we still have people asking about town where the shop is and if we as a couple are still around! But the most important thing is that we had a dream and we had the guts to go for it!

We knew that it was a risk from the offset and that we might fall flat on our faces and lose all the money we had sunk into the shop, but as a couple we sat there and said, "I'd rather go for it and fail than not go for it and always wonder what if!". So that's exactly what we did. We had the perseverance and the industriousness to go for it despite the risks. Yes, we lost the shop but it was through no fault of ours, yes, the shop made money and yes, I have to keep my day job but at least I can stand on my own two feet and look the Gods in the eye and say, "At least I gave it a go!"

SELF RELIANCE

This virtue for all intents and purposes is linked hand in hand to industriousness for it is the ability to rely on one's own initiative and skills to further our own personal lives as well as that of our kin and faith as a whole. Our ancestors believed that regardless of what skill you have it will always find a use within the collective. There would be no use for twenty carpenters and ten builders if no one knew how to thatch! In today's world any skill is not only useful but can act as a psychological tool to spiritual and emotional wellbeing; the very act of learning gives us a sense of worth and also an optimistic vision of our personal futures as well as that of our kin. We must remember that not all our ancestors were warriors. Storytellers, skalds and musicians were all deemed important skills and vital to the tribe in social and spiritual times of trouble.

Freedom as we have discussed is a fundamental to the Heathen Warrior. If we take the time to learn skills we eliminate the need to rely on others (as best as possible) and we can utilise our time more wisely, thus giving us the freedom to live a more positive and productive life. It also gives us the skill set to teach, enrich and pass on that freedom to our children. In the context of the Heathen Warrior this freedom allows us to explore other martial ideas that we may have overlooked or ignored due to the reliance of someone else's teachings. We must question and utilise anything around us that may expand our knowledge and understanding. Obviously the skills you learn may stand you in good stead. For example, if you are far from home in a hostile situation and may be in need of medical treatment, your first aid skills, however small, may very well prove to be the difference between life and death. You don't need to be a doctor with years of experience to help your situation!

"A man should know how many logs

And strips of bark from the birch

To stock in autumn, that he may have enough

Wood for his winter fires".

The Havamal

Personal Example:

I'm going to let you in on a little secret, a secret that will make you chuckle and look at me in a totally different light. I am absolutely useless when it comes to D.I.Y. and home improvements! That's right, when it comes to doing the "traditional" manly arts of tiling, woodwork, plumbing or such I am a disaster waiting to happen! You would of thought that this would prove a major stumbling block and that my wife would be tearing her hair out but you would be wrong. In fact, my ever-patient wife rather likes the fact I am useless in these departments because she loves D.I.Y. and enjoys it so much that she does all the jobs I can't do! Not only is she great at general home improvement jobs but is also a dab hand at everything ranging from Eames taping and plastering to floor laying and carpentry. In fact she is so good she has been asked by friends and family to lend a hand when they are in need of assistance. If asked she will even go as far as saying that she is glad I don't like D.I.Y. because if I did we would have more arguments about who was going to do the job! It is a running joke in the family regarding my lack of skills in this department and just goes to show how reliant I would be if I was on my own.

It would undoubtedly cost me a small fortune to get skilled tradesmen in every time I needed work done but as we can see being self-reliant is not only good for the soul but will save you a ton of money! I think it's time to brush up on my skill set.

PERSERVERENCE

During life we all get knock backs. The time when we think to ourselves "Why me?" or "What have I done to deserve this?" It is as natural as the sky and the wind. It's life, so deal with it! Sorry, it's harsh but true. The ability to dust oneself off and carry on regardless of what has happened and act in the face of adversity is a quality that is bittersweet. I was always told that anything worth having is worth struggling for. I have to say during my younger years I didn't really understand because I knew better and that when I didn't get what I wanted the whole world was out to get me! As I got older I realised that all the falls we have endured have shaped and moulded us into the people we are today. Our hopes, dreams and aspirations are consequences of unattained ambitions.

Our sheer grit and doggedness see us through the tuff times and in turn make the good times all the sweeter; to truly enjoy the fruits of our labour we must first taste bitter defeat. Those who have had everything given to them or have obtained through other means other than hard work give no value to life's successes; it is merely "another" hollow victory. This perseverance has to be utilised in every aspect of our lives. It takes time to learn martial prowess and skill with weapons, to attain enlightenment of the spiritual divine or become a well-rounded, emotionally stable member of our faith. If we were to give up at the first obstacle that lay in our way we wouldn't amount to anything. We would just be "existing" not "living" and would never have the chances to make other mistakes that in turn would help us develop our moral compass, thus allowing us to grow beyond what is expected of us in today's world.

"The generous and bold have the best lives,

Are seldom beset by cares,

But the base man sees bogies everywhere

And the miser pines for presents."

The Havamal

Personal example:

Many years ago when I was sixteen I really didn't have a clue what I wanted to do with my life. Only when I started college did I find something that ticked all the boxes and decided there and then that this is what I was meant to do. The thing I stumbled upon was playing the drums. I loved it and spent many an hour bashing the drum kit in our college music room much to the annoyance of the neighbouring classes. I always remember the drummer from a heavy metal band based at our college being a good musician and my friends and I used to love watching the band play live. When I look back, they never did any live gigs outside the college and were just doing it for fun but I was impressed nonetheless. One day I approached the drummer and asked him for some advice regarding improving my playing (at this point I had only been playing for a couple of months and was terrible), and what he said will stay with me until my dying day and is single handily the most motivational bit of advice I have ever received. It galvanised me into action and made me think, "I will show you. I'm going to be a great drummer!" When I asked him what I should do to improve, he looked at me and with all seriousness said "Quit. You're never going to be as good as me!" I couldn't believe what I heard. He walked away laughing and I walked away thinking, "We will see, sunshine".

So began my drumming career. I slowly got better and my dream was to get a record deal and show the world what I had to offer. Over the next few years I drifted from one band to another honing my skills and getting better and better at my chosen art. Slowly I started to gain a reputation as an awesome metal drummer and soon bands were seeking me out. Disappointment after disappointment, I finally joined a band that seemed to have a special something and after our third demo started to make waves within the heavy metal music industry. Finally, ten years after I started playing I was in the lucky position of being offered a record deal and remember signing the contract in our shared house. It was not to be. Just after signing the deal, tensions regarding the direction of the band came to a head and I decided to leave. At this point I have to say that just like the drummer from all those years ago. I too became arrogant and treated those around me without honour and said some pretty nasty and hurtful things, not to mention acted like a complete fool, and for that I am truly sorry. It was only sometime later I realised what a fool I had been and bridges were built and friendships renewed.

Over the next few years I hooked up with some other ex-members and helped them out with another band. This too started to gain interest from labels but we never took them up on their offers as we felt the deals offered were not to our liking or benefit and to be honest I felt somewhat jaded by the whole music industry. Once again I left the band, but this time due to moving away and a work career. I am pleased to say I am still in touch with the guys and they still play, albeit in different bands. I still play now and again and have taught drums off and on for the last ten years now and still enjoy the buzz from bashing those skins! Regarding bands, you never know what the future may hold.

If that isn't a story for perseverance, I don't know what is. I struggled for ten years to attain my goal and made a lot of sacrifices to get it only to discover that it wasn't all that I thought it would be. I have never made a living out of music but nevertheless I am inwardly proud of myself for never giving in when others were willing me to fail. I attained my goal by sheer determination, self-will and personal perseverance.

As you can see the Nine Noble Virtues are interlinked, entwined and are the very cornerstones of Heathen reasoning and regardless of whether you believe they are a modern invention, no one can argue the ethical standpoint and meaning behind each one. You may agree with some and disagree with others; you may think of other virtues that should join that list or those that should be omitted. Regardless of what you think, the purpose is to be individual and take from it what you will, to ask yourself how they relate to you and how you live your life. In my opinion one virtue basically encompasses all others and if we were all to live our life by that virtue, our world would be a safer and more understanding place. I will let you guess which one it is!

However, no matter how clear the message, there will always be people who will twist it to serve their own evil ambitions and ideals and as a force to dominate others. History has shown us time and time again that when this happens the result can be unspeakable acts of cruelty the likes of which mankind should never see. We as Heathen Warriors must stand and fight those who wish to distort our faith by being of one voice and staying united, regardless of what they say or do.

Chapter Four

Misguided and Misleading

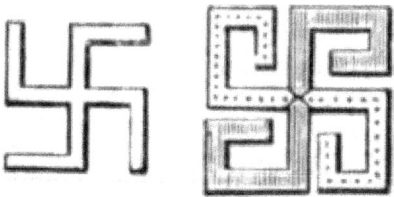

"The fool who fancies he is full of wisdom

While he sits by his hearth at home.

Quickly finds when questioned by others

That he knows nothing at all"

The Havamal

When starting this chapter I was slightly concerned that I wouldn't be able to convey the message to you in an articulate enough way and that the reader would think I was being untruthful or was skirting the issue surrounding the hijacking of my faith, not to mention the dogma faced by a modern Heathen. So I am going to spell it out as straight forward and as pragmatically as I possibly can. I make no apologies if I offend as I honestly believe any morally balanced person regardless of faith would understand my words even if they appear a little dramatic.

Below are what I believe are some basic and moralistic rules all Heathen Warriors should adhere to and some facts regarding my religion that may surprise you. Of course this depends on the level of knowledge you possess regarding the faith and its core fundamentals. With this in mind, I shall presume that you know nothing but the "bad press" regarding our faith.

Please read and re-read as to fully comprehend my words so that there is no doubt left in your mind regarding the true reasoning behind the Heathen Warrior ethos and its relationship to our indigenous faith. Obviously these are my personal ideas; you of course may not agree.

• Under no circumstances should the Heathen Warrior use his/her skill, strength and abilities to bully, intimidate, hurt or put in danger those who are weaker than themselves.

• Everyone regardless of sexual orientation, race or religion deserves to be treated with the respect, honour and humility.

• The Heathen religion is not about a dominant race or the subjugation of any other ethnic peoples.

• The Heathen Warrior will only engage in warfare if he, his family, faith or kin is in danger or to defend the helpless and defenceless in a situation that could cause them harm, and the response should be of equal ferocity to that which is shown.

- Mercy and compassion should be shown if remorse is shown to be genuine. They are to be viewed as qualities not weaknesses.

- Everyone has the right to be proud of their faith, heritage and ancestral home; just because the Heathen Warrior is proud of his does not mean he is racist.

- The most painful forms of true justice are reserved for those who hurt women and children. Violence towards the vulnerable is forbidden.

- Do not confuse passion and loyalty to one's country as bigotry to others.

- Heathen Warriors should respect all others until proved otherwise, regardless of place of origin.

- The Heathen Warrior believes he/she has the right and is legally justified to use force if his/her home is invaded and he/she believes his/her family is in danger.

- It is the ability to keep going, evolving and growing spiritually, emotionally and personally that drives our faith forward.

- A Heathen Warrior must always take responsibility for his/her actions and tend to his/her faith, family and kin with unreserved loyalty and steadfastness.

- By being the best he/she can be the Heathen Warrior ensures that moral brickwork is laid for his/her children's future.

- The Heathen Warrior knows what battles to fight and when it is prudent to retreat and fight another day.

- The Heathen Warrior strives to live by the Nine Noble Virtues and/or the ethos behind each virtue at all times.

- The Heathen Warrior acknowledges he/she will make mistakes but is not only happy but eager to learn from them.

- The Heathen Warrior shall stand and fight shoulder to shoulder if his/her kinsmen are in need and if he/she is in Troth.

- All Oaths shall be honoured and should not be made on a whim.

- The Heathen Warrior whole heartedly agrees with the unwavering fact that our faith is about Heritage not Hate.

- All Heathen Warriors believe it the right of **ALL** peoples to be free from forced doctrines and religious enslavement.

- Freedom is the essence and the force that drives our nation into the future and the governing force in the present.

- True freedom comes with the greatest price of all: sacrifice, discipline and blood.

And the most important statement of all:

Heathenism is not a religion of hate and twisted ideology!

Forgive me for being blunt but I feel my faith has been the target of bad press relations and a sustained campaign of lies and half-truths for too long. Certain groups on the fringes of our ancestral beliefs have distorted and used the Heathen faith as a vehicle for hatred and acts of cruelty, pushing their Aryan agenda to the weak-minded and morally corrupt, using our ancestors' holiest symbols as a rallying focal point for those likeminded fools ready to give themselves to a warped vision of a world that should never be. When we look at it objectively there is a reason these nefarious types hijacked our symbols and the reason is thus. Our ancestors knew full well the immense power that these symbols represent and can channel if used correctly within the magical sense; thus it stands to reason that the "villain" also knew full well the power that our holy symbols invoked and decided to corrupt their meanings and in turn tarnishing the reputation of our beliefs and our magical signs for future generations. We must always be aware that the power that these symbols possess are neutral and it is the will and intent of the user that denotes the outcome of any magical workings conducted. We must always be true of intent when dealing with the magical side of the Northern Traditions and remember that it is not a game and should be treated with respect. These holy symbols have existed for thousands of years and one should always remain diligent regarding their use. I believe it's about time I lent my voice to the growing number of people prepared to set the record straight and stand up as true Heathens, standing tall, proving we are not all the same in defence of the faith we love. I am no academic so I can only tell you in the common tongue and use the words of the working man. True Heathen Warriors are neither Neo-Nazis nor right wing Aryan skinheads crying for ethnic segregation. We do not hate Gays, Lesbians or any other sub-culture. We have no intentions of world dominance and don't want to destroy any other culture. All we ask for is the same rights as other mainstream religions and the freedom to express our faith without the social dogma persecuting us in the media as villains, Satanists and racists. We also want the right to be recognised and acknowledged as a modern, thriving and worthwhile alternative to modern belief systems both in practice and in law, allowing us the same legal protections and rights as others.

Of course as with all religions there will be those who twist the words and beliefs to suit their own warped view of how they think the world should be, but does this mean that the religion itself and all its faithful are guilty by association and inherently flawed? Should all be punished due to the ridiculous views of the minority? Of course history is littered with "good" people doing "bad" things in the name of religion regardless of what faith it is. None of the major religions can say they are without fault. Look at the world around us in the present time. Islamic fundamentalists as well as Christian fundamentalists are distorting their faiths' core values with the aim of religious domination. The fact remains that all belief systems have their extreme followers willing to do harm to others. Some of you reading this book may even have these leanings yourselves and to you I say this: I do not agree with you and in my opinion you are not a Heathen Warrior and do not deserve to be a kinsman of my faith. There are no words in my faith that condone hate or bigotry.

For many years, religion has been corrupted and thrust upon others whom had neither wish nor desire to be "converted" to foreign and to them, alien beliefs. The Heathen Warrior is secure enough in his own spirituality and morality to understand that there is enough room in the world for all religious views. If, however, doctrines are thrust upon them they are fully willing to defend and protect their beliefs without remorse and in my mind fully justified doing so as are all ethnic peoples.

When I was a young man, I was bullied relentlessly at school by others who preyed on whom they believed to be weaker than them. For years I refused to be drawn into petty disputes regarding social stature and as a consequence harboured a hatred for bullies and those who fight and torment others for amusement. At the age of seventeen I started to work as a nightclub doorman and was determined to face my fears and stand up to the people I despised. For fifteen years I worked in this industry and I believe did so in an honourable way; that's not say I didn't make mistakes! I also believe that those years were necessary to ground my anger and make me more accepting of anyone who was different than me. It was an eye-opening experience that I feel had a profound effect on my personal growth both as a person and as a member of our ancestral faith. Today I am proud to say that I have many Gay and Lesbian friends as well as friends from different backgrounds and ethnicities. I see them as fellow human beings with the same flaws, desires and aspirations as me even though we are of different faiths and sometimes don't see eye to eye on other issues; but just because we don't agree on everything does not make us enemies but human beings! I have to say loud and proud that I am honoured to call them friends.

I want to make it perfectly clear that the Heathen Warrior should be tolerant of everyone until proved otherwise. Of course it would be naive to think that we can be friends with everyone and there are people whom I have taken an instant dislike to, where my instinct has screamed, "Watch out!" but that was due to their personality not because of a colour, race or religious reason. It's common sense really isn't it; the Heathen Warriors mantra should be thus: If you come to me showing respect I shall show respect to you in return, but if you come looking for trouble or to harm me or mine then prepare for war!

I don't believe I could be any clearer with regards to my views on this subject; if you have a moral compass and are a balanced person both spiritually and emotionally then you already have the ability to grasp my words and understand their meanings. If however you completely disagree with them then I'm afraid you have serious issues! Of course there will be some of you that completely disagree with me, but to be honest we all have the right to our own opinion, regardless how flawed I believe it to be. But think about this: if you are one of those people who believe that National Socialism is the way forward politically and you call yourself a Heathen and believe in the Nine Noble Virtues, how do you think the Heathen concept of freedom can run hand in hand with the dictatorship that inevitably comes with this type of political system? They are completely at odds with each other and can never be utilized together. So some day you would have to choose. I hope you choose wisely because your decision will not only affect you and your children but the faith as a whole to which you claim to hold dear. Food for thought, I believe.

So let's move on now to a happier subject, a subject that cuts to the quick of the Warrior aspect, the fighting arts and other fun stuff!

Chapter Five

Choose your Weapon – Sword or Briefcase

"Cattle die, kindred die,

Every man is mortal:

But I know one thing that never dies,

The glory of the great dead"

The Havamal

When we are asked, the main thing we all associate when uttering the word "warrior" is the martial arts, fighting styles and the geographical origin of the person concerned. Many scholars used to be under the misconception that our ancestors fighting arts consisted of mindlessly lashing out whilst hoping for the best but that analysis couldn't be further from the truth. Not only did our ancestors develop a sophisticated fighting style utilising a wide variety of weapons, but also a razor-sharp tactical reasoning that served them well in countless conflicts around the globe. Often outnumbered, our ancestors relied on stealth and skill above all-out brawn and readily applied Guerrilla tactics as opposed to open warfare. Of course there were some traditional pitched battles but for the most part surprise and extreme ferocity was the order of business.

When we talk about the warrior path we must also remember that as with many warrior cultures the bond between the warriors was incredible strong and was seen as an absolute unbreakable union before the Norse pantheon. Each warrior was not only responsible for his own life and that of their families but also of that of their fellow warriors. Personal responsibility for staying fit, healthy and up-to-date with fighting techniques and weaponology was encouraged. One has to remember the young age at which some of these warriors were brought into the fold, thus when a boy became of age they had to take part in a rite of passage marking the transition from adolescent to fully fledged Heathen Warrior. Some scholars recount tales of how these rituals took place and of the type of initiation but we must be vigilant to the fact that there is a shortage of concrete evidence to support any credible theory. However, it is generally agreed that a rite of passage was needed to mark a turning point in the young warrior's life. It should also be mentioned that some have suggested homosexuality was ever-present within the warrior cults and to a certain degree I think this theory may have some validation. Even though there is no concrete evidence to suggest such activity within the Heathen Warrior sects, there are a few accounts of homosexuality within the community at large. The general thinking was that as long as the warrior took a wife, raised children and was a dependable warrior and reliable member of the collective then whatever else he got up to in his private life was his own business and had no bearing on his social status within the group or as a warrior. I have to say that this may surprise some of you that such things were acceptable due to the modern day brain washing and ridicule placed upon the stereotypical "macho" image of a warrior and the "girly" unmanly image of homosexuality. It would seem obvious that close bonds were formed between brothers in arms especially when surrounded by so much death and carnage and who's to say with any real certainty that sexual boundaries were not blurred or for that matter even existed at all. One only has to search the history books for evidence of this and can be found some years earlier within the Spartan civilization and warrior way of life. These fearsome and formidable warriors spent their whole lives training for war. Their training started from when they were born and never ceased. It is a known fact that when a young warrior was assigned to an elder for training and education, a sexual bond was also created that was not only accepted but encouraged. The reasoning is such that if an emotional and sexual bond is formed, no man would run from the field of battle and leave one who he has been so intimate with to die. They would rather die together than live in disgrace. Interestingly, the Spartans' wives knew of this bond and were completely at ease with the concept. Whether this was due to social acceptance or enforced doctrines we will never truly know but the fact that it was accepted is a fascinating insight to the Spartan warrior culture. It would appear that attitudes regarding sexuality were far more liberal and socially acceptable before Christianity appeared. There is little doubt that amongst modern scholars and military historians the Spartans are famous for being some of the most skilled warriors in history and I for one wouldn't like to see their sexual activities detract from their ruthlessness and superior attributes on the field of battle. These men should be honoured as heroes and awarded the respect of others, regardless of personal opinion or bigotry.

I and many other Heathens are of the opinion that not only would the young man be forced to swear allegiance to the king or tribal leader but would also have to prove his worth by fighting and possibly beating a veteran warrior in single combat. Only then would the war band know for sure that the initiate was skilful and worthy enough to join the elite group of fighters and thereby securing his place among the tribe and social group. Like many other tribes from around the world I am of the belief that the young man would have to venture out into the wild on his own to travel on his own spiritual journey to commune with the Gods and Goddesses. It would also put his practical skills of bush craft and survival to the test considering the extreme terrain and unpredictability of the harsh northern weather. These skills were not just for show; everyday life was hard and the young warrior used these skills in a dual purpose role. Of course learning to hunt and cook your own food was a talent that served the whole community, not just when they were out travelling the seas to faraway lands. One must also take into account the fact that skinning, bow making, arrow fletching and flint knapping where skills that each young man had been learning and honing all his life and to be anything less than perfect could spell disaster for himself and his kin.

Upon joining the warrior collective, it would also be necessary to choose and bless your weapon as to endow it with supernatural powers, thus giving you a spiritual and psychological advantage in battle. There are accounts that show us some of the names given to such weapons like the Viking who named his axe "skull crusher" or a warrior who named his sword "belly splitter". This may seem strange to the normal folk but as with modern day soldiers they were never far away from their weapon. It was the most precious tool they possessed; a bond was created and as far as our ancestors were concerned the weapon was a living, breathing entity and had to be treated as such. Swords in particular where extremely expensive and generally only the very rich could afford them. Most were passed down as heirlooms and were hugely important and decorative. Magical runes were common along the blade and hilt and poetic verses were also engraved. Unless you had rich kin the chances of owning a sword were slim, but it wasn't uncommon to find one lying on the corpse-strewn battlefield that would be "obtained" as a spoil of war. The primary weapon of choice, however, was the Bearded Axe, followed by the secondary and most universal weapon, the short-bladed knife known as a scramseax (the seax was generally shorter than a sword but longer than a traditional hunting knife). Spears and the Dane axe (a broad axe with a 5-6 foot wooden shaft) were also available and were incredibly dangerous in their own right and were seen as specialist weapons used by highly trained and seasoned warriors.

In today's modern world we have the ability to access the internet and locate reams of information with the click of a button regarding fighting arts from across the globe. Our computer can feed us a constant stream of information regarding modern warfare and its developments as well as that of our distant relatives. It's not surprising then that for the last decade the popularity of Western martial arts has exploded and flourished across the globe. People are realising that the Northern Hemisphere has indeed a lot to offer in the sometimes secretive world of self-defence. I believe it can only enrich and help evolve those arts taught that are the mainstay of every town and city around the world.

In the 21st century there are many groups popping up that train in "Era" and geographical specific styles. This could range from the 18th century sword play of Western Europe as taught by the German masters to early Dark Age Scandinavian spear and axe techniques. All are still relative in the modern world and all have fantastic merits to encompass into our own training regime. The wars and weapons might have changed but the core tactics and mechanics are the same. Every martial art or self defence system has good points and bad points. The long winded and the abstract techniques can cause confusion and sometimes hinder a student's progress; the trick is to master what is useful and discard what isn't. As I have said before I am of the personal opinion that less is more; a handful of repeatedly drilled techniques is of more use than 100 semi-learnt!

The warrior aspect ultimately revolves around the fact that even though we possess the skills to defend our family and friends we must have the ability to temper our emotions so that it does not become a hindrance and affects our spirituality in a detrimental way. All the power in the world is useless without the means to control it; if we fail to control and focus our skills we inevitably become like the people we deem are without a moral compass, thus losing our honourable place among our family and kin not to mention our faith.

I have to stress that as a Heathen Warrior I feel it is our duty and responsibility to learn some sort of self defence system to at least some level of proficiency. The main reasoning for this is six-fold:

▪   To have the ability to protect yourself, family, kin and faith in the advent of a violent confrontation.

▪   To instil a sense of self-discipline regarding ALL aspects of our lives.

▪   To help develop one's emotional and spiritual outlook regarding the world around us.

▪   To help with relaxation from today's hectic world.

▪   To give ourselves something to aspire to and the gratification of attaining goals.

▪   To create a bond between our ancestors and ourselves in the present.

Of course there are loads of other benefits but I deem these as the main ones appertaining to our faith.

I often get asked what the best fighting art is and it's a question that does not have a definitive answer but rather a subjective one. I have been involved with martial arts for most of my life and asking such a question is like asking how long a piece of string is! There will be people who advocate certain systems and ridicule others but please make your own mind up! Having trained in many disciplines over the years, I personally believe you should first start with western boxing and use it as a foundation. You don't have to compete or become a world champion (unless you want to!), but the core fundamentals of body mechanics are second to none. I found this out at a later stage in my martial arts journey and often wish I had started all those years ago! It also teaches you impeccable timing and the correct way to throw a punch without causing yourself an injury, a vital skill in any violent confrontation. It is also great for fitness. I would also personally recommend you try some of the following and see what suits you.

Israeli Krav Maga Self-Defence System

A highly effective form of street self-defence originally designed for the Israeli military. No fancy moves just explosive power. The aim is to hit hard and fast, then get out of the area. I myself have trained in this art and personally rate it highly.

Muay Thai – Thai Kickboxing

A devastating Thai art utilising knee and elbow strikes, as well as kicks and punches. Mainly used as a sport, but there are applications not allowed in the ring that can be utilised in a street attack.

Russian Submission SAMBO Wrestling

Crippling self-defence system incorporating locks, pins, throws and bone-breaking techniques! I have had the opportunity to train a little in this art and have to say I well and truly got my bottom kicked! Very effective and highly enjoyable.

MMA Training (Mixed Martial Arts)

This is everything covered in one place including Western boxing, Ju-Jitsu and a variety of other disciplines. A new breed of fighter has emerged over the last ten years utilising MMA. As with Muay Thai, it is manly used in the ring; however it is extremely useful in the real world.

Any European Martial Arts club

These are harder to find and focus on traditional weapons such as sword, axe, spear, knife, shield, etc. It is good fun and adds to the training roster. It also keeps a link to our faith system.

This is not a definitive list and there are loads of other martial arts out there so I suggest you see what is happening in your local area and attend a few classes, thus giving you a clear idea of what each discipline is about and whether you see yourself enjoying it. Don't forget that the idea is not only to evolve and grow but to have fun. If we don't enjoy what we do then we are wasting energy that could be put to use in another venture. Focus your talents on an art you truly rate regardless of what others say to you. Regardless of how long it takes, please don't rush or try to find a quick fix solution or jump at the first class you see. Take your time and really think about the choices you have. We should remember that whatever we learn should not be used to bully and intimidate those weaker than us. We should only use it if we have no other choice and when we do, we do so without remorse or guilt, for the Heathen Warrior believes that if he/she has been forced to use such force we are totally justified in our actions. Of course apart from defending their homes or going to war there were other times in which our ancestors thought it was not only right to fight but wholly pragmatic in an effort to save lives

Einvigi and Holmgang

As we know in our ancestors' era, honour played a major role in their daily lives and disputes were common between different tribes. If conflicts arose they would have a choice between open warfare or of a slightly different course of action. For years there existed a form of duel known as Einvigi. This was a duel of single combat without any governing rules that could be fought anywhere and everywhere and had absolutely no restrictions on the type of weapon used. However this proved to be as expensive as all-out war would be. The last thing a chieftain would want is to lose all his best men in some dispute thus leaving his village at the mercy of raiders; likewise an unregulated duel could also prove expensive and problematic due to the unpredictability of the duel itself. No one really knew what was happening and if lost, monies would have had to be given to the winning side. As a result, our ancestors decided that a new form of duel be devised that still had the power to settle disputes but was more controllable. Thus Holmgang was invented. This form of single combat was fought in a roped-off square and each warrior had three shields. It was the right of the accused or insulted man to have first strike. Any weapon could be used but historians believe that the main ones where sword and axe. The clever thing about the duel was that once blood had been spilt the match was considered over; however, it regularly ended in mortality due to the fact that when you swing an axe at full force it generally takes a head off! Nevertheless, if you didn't kill your opponent and just wounded him at least you still won. It is also generally agreed that the loser had to pay the winner monies, the sum of which was agreed upon at the beginning of the match and held onto by a neutral observer. There are some accounts of people running out of the square and giving in before a blow was even thrown! I am of the opinion that this sort of behaviour was far and few between based on the fact that so much emphasis was placed on the warrior culture and not to mention the fact that your Orlog (personal doom explained later in another chapter) would be in tatters and to your kin you would be a man of no worth and honour. In addition, you would lose all social standing within the community. It also stands to reason that those involved in said duel were very capable warriors and had been for some time and were fully aware of the duties expected of them and the consequences of not getting it right. It may seem barbaric but this was not seen as merely entertainment but a practical way to settle disputes. It saved a lot of lives and of course, money. One only has to look at the Roman Empire and the role gladiators played to find more evidence of the notion that people are drawn to blood sports and that the warrior culture has existed throughout the ages.

Of course in the modern age no such duelling to the death exists in any civilized country. However, there are new sports that push the boundaries and contain the same premise as to that of the ancient duel. There is the sweet science known as boxing, but it has seen a demise in popularity in recent years due to another new sport rearing its gladiatorial head. In today's modern age the sport of Mixed Martial Arts or cage fighting has taken off in a big way, attracting audiences from all over the world. I must admit that my friends and I enjoy watching our favourite fighters engage in single combat. People have brandished the sport barbaric and nothing but an unregulated blood sport but I feel it not only takes great skill but complete fear draining guts to enter the cage and engage another man face to face. It is honourable and separates those who want from those that wish. There is always mutual respect from the fighters which I applaud in today's immoral world. You may wonder why I mention this but here is the twist. I myself have been involved and asked if I had any desire to fight, but I declined and my reasoning is thus: I cannot truly switch on my "killer" instinct just for sport. It has to be a very real and life-threatening event to activate me properly. In the cage the other man wants to hurt me but when all is said and done there are still rules to which both sides abide to. In real life of course, no such rules exist and when you are fighting for your life against a person who is attacking you with the sole intent of killing or seriously harming you or your family ......anything goes and deserves no remorse. Of course I would love to say this is an extreme example but unfortunately senseless acts of violence are becoming more and more prevalent across the globe, hence the need for educating yourself and your family.

As a footnote to emphasise my point regarding sports fighting and real self-defence there is a fantastic quote given by Lord Eddard Stark, a character in the superb Game of Thrones television series. When approached by a formidable fighter who is excited by the prospect of engaging in single combat with Lord Stark, Stark responds that he does not partake in competitions. His foe is somewhat bemused and asks why, to which Stark simply replies, "When I fight a man for real I don't want him to know what I am capable of". When I heard this I couldn't help but smile. Wise words that we can all learn from.

Alongside the martial arts I feel it is imperative that the Heathen Warrior cultivates as many different skills as possible, not only that could prove invaluable in times of emergency, civil unrest, war, social and economic breakdown, disaster or everyday life, but to enrich our sense of freedom and self-reliance. The act of broadening our horizons and learning in itself makes us feel like a productive member of our family and social group and the discipline required to acquire said skills enrich us both emotionally and spiritually. Please do not confuse or misinterpret the reasoning behind learning these skills. The aim is not to become and develop a "paranoid survivalist" mentality but rather a "hope for the best, plan for the worst" mind-set and world view. Looking back at the virtue of self-reliance and the quote from *The Havamal,* it says that we should be prepared for the coming winter. Would it not make sense that we apply such reasoning to everything around us and towards planning for any problem that may present itself? Of course this is not to say that we should waste all of today worrying about tomorrow or that we should lock ourselves away in fear of the unknown, but to me it is prudent that we at least make reasonable plans to limit our exposure rather than leave it to chance or even worse, stick our heads in the sand screaming "I'm not listening!" in fear of being labelled paranoid! It is also important to point out that we are all unique and learn at different rates and excel at different things, so don't beat yourself up if you are not a natural at some of the skills or take a longer time to become proficient. Remember, perseverance! Our ancestors knew that the warrior had to develop certain skills that would not only serve them well in the face of battle but would also enrich their folk and the daily struggle that they faced.

The R.V.A Principal

On a personal note: Over the years I have come to believe that when learning a new skill or expanding my creativity, one important component is a mind-set I call The R.V.A. system. This system can be applied to every aspect of the Heathen Warrior ethos, from martial training to magical workings.

R.V.A. is a simple three step program for attaining our desires.

Realisation – Visualisation – Actualisation

REALISATION

This is basically "waking" up to our current situation, admitting our failings and being truly honest with ourselves regarding were we are in life and where we want to go. The key is to be brutally honest with our intentions and not to sugar-coat or to make excuses for why we haven't achieved before. We have to quietly contemplate, find a tranquil place and cleanse before we can take the next step. A full cup cannot take any more water.

VISIUALISATION

See in our minds-eye the desired outcome and focus on the finish line rather than worry about the journey itself. We must see ourselves achieving said dream or completing a chosen project and basking in the self-satisfaction that we made it, and that we did it on our own without assistance. A victory born out of hard work, toil and sacrifice tastes a damn sight better than being given it on a plate! Prepare for the journey and give it 100% of your energy; give it your all or go home!

ACTUALISATION

Actually achieving your goal and all the riches that come with it! This could be financial, spiritual or emotional. Only YOU can put a price on this achievement and for the most part it is a personal sense of pride and fulfilment that will be your reward. You have worked hard and now is the time to enjoy the spoils of that dedication.

It may seem like common sense but it is easier said than done when life throws all it's got at you in a defiant display of power! This is when the Nine Virtues really come into being and give you the driving force to attain greatness.

Whilst we are on the subject of learning new skills here are some skills you may not have thought about that may prove useful during our time here on Midgard and will give you a sense of self-worth and a feeling of pride, not to mention the opportunity to test your new found R.V.A mind-set! Apart from the obvious benefits of self-reliance and preparedness they will also teach us among other things, hand eye coordination and skills from which to earn a living should we wish a career change and let's not forget, give us a link to our ancestors and the skills they possessed.

▪   Firearms, Archery, First Aid, Fire Fighting, Cooking, Self-Reliance, Growing your own Food, Gardening, Bush Craft, Orienteering, Climbing, Driving, Diving, Leather Craft, Clothes Making, Flying, Hunting, Flint Knapping, Building, Carpentry, Plumbing, Thatching, Tele-communications .

Of course this is not meant to be an exhaustive list but an aid to fire off your own imagination with regards to the amount of things available to us to learn and experience. Anything you feel can be of use to yourself, the family or tribe is to be considered valuable and should be explored with vigour and relish.

Self-sufficiency is also a skill to be nurtured and encouraged amongst our folk in the sense of growing our own food, raising livestock and tending to our own little piece of land. If we engage all our family and folk in such activities we build bonds and the basis for a Heathen community. This also helps to project a hardworking and environmental image of what our faith is about to those not involved or unaware of our belief system. We must educate our young the real meaning of freedom and arm them with the facts regarding where our food really comes from. I myself would love to be in the position one day of owning a little bit of land so that I could sink my own water well, erect my own green wind turbine, grow my own vegetables and even have chickens supplying eggs to my kitchen! Alas in the modern age rural property and land is extremely expensive here in England. In the old days everyone wanted to live in the towns and cities to show their wealth but now the money people buy up all the country property to escape city life forcing the property prices up, thus forcing the local countryside people into the city due to the fact they can't afford the properties where they grew up! It is a shame because most of the time the city dwellers only use the properties as holiday homes and only visit occasionally. There is, however, a few places in Scotland where property and land are still relatively cheap compared to the rest of the country. But ironically we would be the outsiders and "city dwellers", entering a community where the locals could not afford to buy. This happened to me when I moved to the Isle of Lewis, an island off the west coast of Scotland. I did meet my wife there so it wasn't all bad!

It is also not only beneficial but imperative to have a trade or skill from which to generate income in such areas. This is due to the fact of high unemployment and lack of work. It will open doors for you from which one can enter and participate in the local underground economy. Arty, crafty skills and talents are best for these types of situations. Tourists like locally made crafts and in summer months can generate some good earnings to see you through the economically harsher winter months. My own wife is an extremely talented artist and is well known for her amazing animal portraits, but she also had stalls at local markets and gatherings selling her handmade arts and crafts. She still paints and sells her work to this day even though we are now in England. There are a lot of bartering projects popping up all over the place now; in Glastonbury, England for example there exists a growing favour for a favour mentality. No money is exchanged, only a mutually beneficial exchange. I will fix your fence if you give me some eggs! In my opinion this is fantastic progression in social trends and should be utilised and encouraged more across the country. It is not only returning us to a tribal way of doing things but bringing us spiritually closer to our ancestors, as well as shedding the importance of money to the annoyance of the tax stealing "big brother" state!

As you can see the self-reliance and learning of new skills stands us in good stead when all the pieces are placed together.

But before you get too cosy, there are pitfalls. One must be aware that the governments both here in the U.K. and in America are trying to push ridiculous laws into place that restrict our rights regarding growing our own food and supplying our own homes with our own amenities. They wish to tax car boot sellers, egg sellers, as well as the man on the side of the road selling strawberries! They even have their beady little eyes on eBay!

All humour aside, may I suggest you look on the internet and do your own research for information regarding these new draconian laws because I and many others feel they not only stand in the way of our warrior path but infringe on our civil liberties, not to mention our human rights!

When talking about the battles we face as a warrior we are not just confining ourselves to the face to face physical confrontations, but rather a variety of situations that can present themselves in our daily lives. Regardless of social placement, we all face our own trials and tribulations and all react in different ways; however how we react reveals a lot about our character and the inner workings of our being. Every day we are bombarded with choices and dilemmas that have the potential to cause conflict through no fault of our own. This could range from road rage to our boss treating us like a child in front of our co-workers, thus stirring our inner warrior and letting it scream to be unleashed. In such circumstances we must be prudent in our reactions and not let our warrior nature run amok. We need to provide for our families and if we lose our composure, even just for a second, we run the risk of placing hardship upon our kin and the ones we love. Having said that, one must always remain assertive and be prepared to stand our ground if we believe we are in the right and if we feel that we are being unjustly treated; in this instance temperance and cunning need to be employed and all the facts ascertained before stating your case. No matter how big the mountain faced, with perseverance and fortitude the truth will always win over tyranny.

Every warrior carries his /her own weapon. Be it briefcase or sword it matters not in today's age; even at the total opposites of the spectrum we discover that the same fundamentals apply. Let us take the highly paid business man for example, entering the office for that really important big-money meeting, ready to negotiate, hoping for the opportunity to walk away with a substantial and life-altering deal is for all intents and purposes using the same mental fortitude and Heathen Warrior energy as the man in the factory who sweeps the floor. Because the floor sweeper knows he is worth more, but nevertheless endures his day to day monotony, minimum wages and the ridicule of those above him who believe them to be better than him for the sake of his family. Self-pride and dignity is to be cherished. It is a shame in the modern age success is measured by wealth. I truly believe that regardless of how many "things" you own or how many zeros are listed on your bank balance it is true happiness and a sense of self-worth that defines our success in life. Being surrounded by people you love and who love you in return is the most rewarding gift a warrior can possess.

Chapter Six

Family, Faith and Kin

"If you know a friend you can fully trust,

Go often to his house

Grass and brambles grow quickly

Upon the untrodden track"

The Havamal

So then, as Heathen Warriors why do we do it? why do we strive to be better and become all we can be in this crazy world we call home? Why do we hold on to our rock in stormy waters? Why do we stand firm in the face of adversity and ridicule from the outside world? Why do we stay true to our beliefs when others do not understand us or believe we are something we are not? The answer is simple: Family, Faith and Kin.

As we have discovered we all face life's ups and downs with varying results and as Heathen Warriors it is of upmost importance that we must face all trials and tribulations head on whilst standing on our own two feet, proud and with complete resolve in our belief system. We must enjoy every moment of everyday and try to make the most of the time that we are given, for none of us truly know how long we have on Midgard or when the Gods bid us to travel to Valhalla. The simple pleasures that this world has to offer are better for sharing with those that are closest to us. Spending quality time with those we love should be paramount and regardless of how busy our lives are, time should always be set aside for family gatherings. We don't need to spend vast sums of money and it is not about huge events but rather quality time when we actually listen to each other and make time for each other and unify the bonds between us. We must remember that family are our crutch in troubling times and as they are there for us, we are there for them. We must never forget that as a family unit we triumph together or fail together; thus honesty and total trust must be paramount within the close family unit and to kin.

When we take a closer look at our faith it is obvious that it is so interwoven within our daily lives that it is almost impossible to separate any issue without dissecting the dynamics of how we Heathen Warriors interact with others. Any belief system advocates the family unit but I truly believe that our ancestors hit the "mother lode" with regards to the family unit within the tribal context. Of course this is not to say we can't learn from anyone else and that we have it completely sussed but at least we can say, "I'm doing my best but I can always learn more"!

This I believe separates our indigenous belief system from other religions; the fact that we can admit our possible short falls is in my opinion a testament to our ancestors and the tolerance of our faith in the modern world. As we are all aware we must evolve and adapt to the 21st century or face the possibility of fading in the mists of time.

I can only explain from my point of view based on information and knowledge gathered from my own experiences and others who share my faith within my inner circle. I truly believe that as Heathen Warriors representing our faith we must above all else seek to provide the safest environment for our children to be raised in with the highest emphasis placed upon emotional and spiritual development, for they are the future ambassadors of our faith. Our aim should not be for them to be shut off from the rest of the world and insular, but rather advocate the exploration of it, to seek out knowledge whenever possible and to experience and enjoy the pleasures midgard has to offer. To stifle and "brainwash" serves no purpose and will ultimately have an adverse effect; the only result to imprint a narrow minded view on an innocents mind thus creating a self-fulfilling prophecy that would spell doom for our faith. I truly believe that our faith is balanced and moralistic regarding today's confusing and morally dubious world, therefore arming our children with the correct tools they will need when venturing out on their own. When out on their own their values and more importantly, actions, will be the benchmark of how our faith interacts with others. It will, in my opinion, act as a beacon, thus illuminating the populous at large and showing the true aspects of our faith rather than the idea that all us Heathens are huddled in one dark place with the desire to remain isolated from the world around us. By their actions and deeds, not by preaching, more people will start to look at our indigenous faith with renewed interest instead of scepticism and suspicion.

As parents it is our duty to encourage growth, discipline when necessary and praise often our young when they are in those important years of childhood. As we all know it is a minefield growing up and the world throws many temptations in our path, and the fact that the world is changing at an alarming rate only compounds the problem. There exists dangers in today's world that were unheard of in my younger years and if you are older, some that weren't around in your day! Today's materialistic world is more wealth-orientated than I can ever remember and pose a very real issue when raising children. When our children see others with all the latest gadgets and families that are struggling in the economic downturn in an effort to shower their offspring with presents to ease the guilt of working longer and longer hours just to keep the wolf from the door, thus spending no quality time with their children, we must be cruel to be kind; to give in and hand over all they desire would be dire and could lead to serious ramifications in the future. Children from an early age must be encouraged that they must work for what they want in life and that the world does not owe them a living! However, we must also try to allow them to be children as long as possible for it is these years that denote social interaction skills and their character development, affecting them in the future.

Encouragement must be ever present during our children's formative years; we must educate but allow free thought thus helping to nourish the seeds of individuality. They must be allowed to ask questions and question why we respond in a certain way. Each child will have their own unique characteristics, skills and attributes, each as fragile as they are different. Our guidance is paramount and our protection of our offspring unwavering but to stifle will only cause them to pull away from us thus driving them to the dangers from which we seek to shield them. However, a balance must be developed and boundaries drawn between the child and the adult. The pleasure we as parents get from our children's triumphs are indescribable as too are their disappointments but as we all know by now these bad times make the victories all the sweeter!

I am a firm believer that our children should be free of our own desires for them in their future years. We should abstain from using them as a vehicle for our own regrets or shortfalls in life and should be allowed to follow their dreams without fear of ridicule or complaint from those who profess to love them unconditionally. It is after all their life to do so as they please; however, our wisdom should always be available to guide them should they have need of it. If we have succeeded in our moralistic teachings our children will understand and respect the wisdom that we possess and in turn they may pass on the faith to their young. However, we must be prepared for the chance that some children in their later years may want to rebel against the faith and seek out alternatives; it may not be to our liking but we have to abide by their decision. We must stand true to our faith and ideals of freedom and let them make their own way. It may prove a bitter pill to swallow but a pill swallowed none the less. What kind of parent would we be to stand in the way of our child's happiness? Isn't that what we want for our kids?

As they grow older and if we have done our job right as parents, our children will have a strong sense of identity, a robust work ethic and most importantly, a moral compass. As long as they strive to be the best they can be and to live happy and productive lives whilst treating others with respect, then as far as I am concerned we have succeeded in raising a man or woman worthy of our faith regardless of what they do for a living, sexual orientation or religious view. To be proud of our offspring and to love them without question is in my opinion a testament to our faith and a vindication to those who falsely believe our religion is nothing more than a fantasy of the far right and stands tall amongst other faiths that are less tolerant of those that are different. I am honoured to count myself amongst those who call themselves Heathen Warriors, both past and present, and believe that just like the skalds writing of our ancestors future skalds will pass on our faith with joyous hearts.

The skaldic traditions, the skills of storytelling and of song passed from father to child, one generation to another were also the means to spread news between tribes and not to mention used for good old fashioned entertainment! In the Heathen Warrior ethos it is important to keep such traditions alive. I have done this by educating my daughter to the best of my ability and encouraging her to explore her artistic skills. I have to say she has her mother's gift regarding art and is an amazing artist as well as a keen reader, actor and singer. At present she is excelling at school and enjoys debating world views and politics! I am so very proud to say that she is developing into a very balanced and morally correct young lady. I would love to take the whole credit but I think her mother would object! Joking aside, that's the whole point; we must encourage our children to explore art in all its forms, to learn to express themselves and our beliefs through all avenues open to us. A play, a painting or a piece of music may survive years after we are gone and just like our ancestors, leave a record of tales of daring or just the day to day lives of the family unit. This by its very definition will make us immortal and we will live forever in the hearts and minds of those who come after us as we do now thinking about our ancestors. If we learn by our ancestors' mistakes then it stands to reason that future generations will learn from ours, thus allowing our faith to grow and evolve. My contribution to the skaldic tradition is the written word; this is mainly due to the fact that my artwork is terrible and I have an atrocious singing voice! Our ancestors did not have a written record of their lives at first so the emphasis was placed on poem and song; the written word appeared much later in the form of the Eddas and other historical documents. As I have stated, I feel it is imperative that records of our beliefs, values and lives be recorded in some form or another and who better than our children to carry that flame?

The bonds that bind those of us within our close circle are incredible strong and should be able to withstand immense force and the pressures of modern living. As a united family unit we are stronger than any one warrior standing alone, thus creating a stable environment not just for the young but for every member of the tribe. Social wellbeing and emotional gratification are also key factors incorporated within the tribal unit. The combined family support structure acts as a spiritual magnifier thus unifying the members and strengthening bonds between all concerned. Grandparents, parents, friends and children all have their own part to play within the Heathen community. Everyone within the unit will have a specific role depending on their skill set but all are willing to learn new skills and to evolve as the tribe sees fit. All will band together in times of need and it is expected that each do their bit in the day to day workings and to help out within the family unit regardless of age or social status.

Just because I'm the warrior doesn't mean I get let off from doing some housework!

It is also important to mention that as Heathens we should endeavour that the family home should be a place of peace and tranquillity. We should always try to separate our work life from our home thus offering all within the close family unit a place of sanctuary from the troubling times outside in the world. A balanced, loving home creates a spiritual vortex brimming with Heathen energy and the overwhelming feeling of joy gifted to us from the Gods and Goddesses on high in which we as Heathen Warriors utilise to recharge our optimism regarding our faith and life itself, passing it on to our family. Such energy can take on a life of its own; it is organic and may still remain a long time after you have passed to another realm. If you have ever visited a property with the view to purchase a new home, you may have been aware that sometimes you can feel the residual energy left by the previous family, be it good or bad, thus effecting your decision to buy or not. It stands to reason that such an environment within our home and its surrounding energy magnifies and reinforces the bonds between us and our children, letting them flourish in their early years and aiding them to evolve and grow into worthwhile members of our faith, not to mention cementing the bonds between parents and children. If the energy within the home is of a stable and loving nature the family dynamic works without any real effort. It develops its own natural flow creating a "we" mentality rather than a "I" viewpoint, thus strengthening bonds not just within the immediate family but with kin and friends and all who are invited in to share home and hearth. Of course this has a knock-on effect when your visitors leave and return to their own homes or tribes. This ever expanding spiritual energy has the power to unify our nation and with others who are open enough to listen and embrace it. I will elaborate further regarding the magical use within the Heathen Warriors ethos in a later chapter. But be aware that such a gift is precious and we should always be cautious of others whom we have never dealt with before.

The Old and the Wise

"Never laugh at the old when they offer counsel,

Often their words are wise:

From shrivelled skin, from scraggy things

That hand among the hides

And move amid the guts,

Clear words often come"

The Havamal

Whilst on the subject of family and kin special mention has to be given to the elders, not just within our faith but in our communities as a whole. I don't think that I am alone in saying that those of my age, regardless of faith, were raised to show respect to those older than us, especially the elderly. Within our tradition it is an absolute rule that these people should been treated with respect and humility, not just for the sacrifices they have made for the folk but for the knowledge they possess. Of course during our ancestors' time the life expectancy wasn't that impressive so if someone did survive to old age it was seen as a major achievement and should be treated as such. Nowadays, however, our society as a whole has the reverse attitude; it seems like once you get to old age you are no longer worth anything to the social collective, thereby being left on the scrap heap or left to rot in an old peoples' nursing home full of so-called nurses that have no time to spend with them. I realise that there are a lot of good people out there that do a vast array of good work and are trying to get things improved but as a general rule elders are left to decay and wait for their life to end, even though they have been productive and tax-paying members of society all their lives. On a personal note, I am truly disgusted at the way these folk are treated and am not looking forward to my older years for I fear the state our health service and our economy will be in and whether it will be able to look after me properly. I strongly urge all of you to just remember those left in limbo and if you can help please do so, for you never know when you will need the help.

Friends and Charitable Work

When it comes to friends, less is more. I personally have a small circle of friends to whom I am extremely loyal and expect that same loyalty in return. They know they are welcome at my door anytime and that I would give them my last pound if I could. I believe that this kind of loyalty is a rare commodity in this day and age; very few people can say they have true friends. They may have a vast array of acquaintances but would they help you in times of real danger? My guess is that you could only count on one hand the amount of true friends they have. Friendship of course is like a flower, delicate at first but with time and experience it grows into something worthwhile and beautiful. We must be thankful of true friends and never take advantage of them when they are in need of our help; to do so goes against the very nature of our bonds and the Gods won't be happy! A lot of people say they believe in these ideals but in my bitter experience, they run and save their own skin rather than stand and fight (whatever the battle may be). It is easy to run your mouth about loyalty and honour but a lot harder to back it up when it all goes wrong!

I have to admit that as Heathens, being sociable is a double edged sword. I personally like the company of very close friends. I enjoy sitting around an open fire chatting and sharing food and drink but also enjoy my own company, thus creating a contradiction! Most of my Heathen friends are a lot more sociable than I but they accept my ways and never force anything upon me. So the message is clear: even though we are all Heathens we still have some individual traits and they should be encouraged regardless of personal views.

Even though we are Heathens I am a strong believer that we should never turn away someone who genuinely needs our help. It would be folly to say that we must help everybody due to the fact that it would be logistically impossible; however I encourage all Heathen Warriors to do some sort of charitable work within their own community and immediate area. Some would argue that charity begins at home and I have to admit I agree with that statement to a certain degree. As far as I am concerned as long as you help someone you are doing something right and it's not the amount you do but the intent behind such action. Not only does it show our faith in a good light but helps sooth the soul and gives us a sense of self-worth. It is completely up to you in what form this takes. If you like animals why not donate some time to your local shelter or buy some food for the animals to help stretch the shelter's finances further? If you have an old folk's home near you why not pop in and make cups of tea for a few hours, maybe even volunteer to run a bingo night?

The choice is yours. There are no hard and fast rules. I understand some of you may say, "I'm too busy" or "I haven't got time to fit it all in", but when you live such a hectic lifestyle and contribute regardless, that's when the Orlog truly comes into its own and replenishes your soul with vital spiritual and emotional energy. As Heathen Warriors, don't be fooled into thinking that we must appear macho and warrior-like all the time, as history has shown us it is not a weakness to care for others and give a little help without gaining anything in return. A life spent helping others is not a wasted life.

Charity is obviously a personal choice and I am not for one second telling you what to do and how to live your life, but when all is said and done those who go out of their way to help others regardless of what form it takes give out the true essence of the Heathen Warrior and in return gain spiritual Orlog in way of payment. Don't get me wrong; I am not suggesting we take part in acts of random kindness just to boost the balance of our karma bank but it has to be mentioned nonetheless. Throughout history there has always existed a band of warriors who take part in social and community events to help those less fortunate. From Japanese samurai to the knights of medieval Europe it was not only seen as noble and honourable but looked upon as a civic duty towards and for the greater community. I am of the opinion that these modern times have made us lose sight of such traditions and have left the bitter taste of materialism in our mouth. It's about time we regained that honourable trait in time enough to actually remember what having a moral compass and social conscious is all about.

Just remember, Odin sometimes walks among us disguised as a poor man begging for change. Just a thought to get you thinking.

Chapter Seven

Valkryies and Shield Maidens

"Never seduce another's wife,

Never make her your mistress"

The Havamal

Another misconception regarding our faith is the view that it is a misogynistic belief system with little regard to the feminine aspect, but this could not be further from the truth.

Our ancestors were extremely aware that our wives and women folk played just as, if not a more important role within our lives than that of the men. Not only were the women in charge of the home and expected to do the traditional "womanly" jobs like raising the children, cooking, textiles, washing, etc., but were also expected to defend and fight to the death if necessary when the menfolk where away. Some scholars say there is no historical evidence to support this; however, I believe it would have had to be an absolute necessity when we take into consideration the length of time the menfolk would be away and the level of hostilities during this period. The women knew very well the fate that awaited them should the village be attacked by raiders or enemies of the tribe whilst the men were absent; thus in my opinion making them fight twice as hard and with a complete rage that would send a shiver down the spine of any self-respecting Heathen Warrior! This theory is controversial within the academic world but I and many others believe our ancestors would have been pragmatic and common sense would of prevailed. I'm sure they wouldn't have left the womenfolk unprotected and unprepared. There are other accounts throughout history that show us that women are just as capable fighting in battle as the men. Just look at Boudicca!

Within the community, women were on the whole shown respect unless they brought great shame or disgrace upon the family or tribe as a whole. They were seen as life bringers, gifting the tribe with sons and daughters whom in turn would carry the faith into the future. Of course if our ancestors acquired slaves from various raids on enemy villages then they were fair game for anything they deemed fit. Even though it was barbaric, it was commonplace during the early medieval period and carried on many years into the future by many ethnic peoples from all corners of the world, including the more "civilized" ones.

Our ancestors believed that most women within their tribe not only possessed great spiritual and magical powers due to the miracle of childbirth but some were regarded as a seeress, as healers and as spiritual conduits to the other realms, keepers of the shamanic magic known as seidr, and experts regarding the mysteries of the runes. These magical women went by the name volva. Incidentally, magic was seen as a predominately female endeavour in specific areas of northern Europe and amongst Heathen tribes ranging from Iceland to Denmark, but there are records showing men following this path without entertaining the Warrior aspect. I am of the opinion that they are intertwined and must be studied together. One must be able to protect oneself, family and kin on this level as well as in the spiritual realm, and I am a strong advocate of the traditional. If you are interested in this I suggest you purchase a book specifically dealing with Northern Shamanic Magic. I shall, however, be mentioning this topic again later.

Over the last few centuries it has been well documented that women have been fighting an uphill battle for equal rights in every aspect of modern living and in my opinion they have every right to do so. I don't believe for a second that men are superior in any way, shape or form to that of the fairer sex; in fact I would go as far to say that I believe that women are far more resilient and determined than men in pretty much all circumstances that present themselves.

Of course in modern times there seems to be the start of a bit of a backlash against the feminist movement and a revival of what some believe to be "traditional" values. More and more women seem to express the desire to return to the 1950's viewpoint that the woman should stay at home and the man should go out and earn the money. However, in today's economical challenging times it seems they may not have a choice due to the high cost of living. Ever increasingly, both partners must share the duties equally out of necessity rather than choice. Ironically this is the way our ancestors lived thousands of years ago. Maybe they knew what was coming or maybe they weren't as primitive as the history books suggest.

If we take a close look at the major religions around the world there seems to be an overwhelming intolerance to women within the faiths and in some instances they even take on the role of second class citizen. Islam, for example, is renowned for its subjugation and brutal treatment of women while some denominations of Christianity who profess to be "more tolerant than that of the other faiths" refuse to have women as vicars or priests. I, as well as many of my Heathen folk, find it alien that in this day and age women are still treated this way and that a so called "faith" could be responsible for the reasoning and justification behind such draconian logic. As I have stated elsewhere in this book, it would appear there are extremists everywhere regardless of the religion and landmass it originates from whose views seem to be at odds with any free thinking, morally balanced human being. I would like to stress that it is not my intention to attack or belittle certain other faiths but merely to highlight the different attitudes regarding the role of women within the Northern Tradition. Our religion cares about civil rights for all its followers, not just those of the male variety and the notion of free speech is an absolute and fundamental right regardless of whether you agree with me or not.

If one takes a deeper look or for that matter a quick internet search regarding the faith and the pantheon of deities associated with the belief system of the Northern Hemisphere, we can immediately recognise that there is a multitude of Goddesses as well as Gods. Each with a semi-specific role within the religion and with varying attributes, skill sets and motivations. It would appear that the realms of the deities mirror that of our world here on earth, with mothers, fathers, sons and daughters and even including family dramas, deception, betrayal and other situations more akin to our own family and human structures than that of a race of all-knowing beings. It stands to reason that we as followers of the faith must at least try to honour all the Gods and Goddesses at some point or in some way or another (even just a quick "Hail!" does them good and puts a smile on their face!), even though we might have an affinity with a specific deity. We must bear in mind that we must always strive to utilise whatever deity is appropriate for our individual purpose at that given time and that can relate to the task at hand, providing us with the outcome we desire. The Gods and Goddesses are aware that we may not need them all the time and are reluctant to get involved with matters that are not within their skill set; however just because they are mainly regarded as being dominant in a certain field, looks can be deceiving. Freyja, for example, is mainly associated with fertility but is a formidable warrior and can rival any God within the pantheon in combat. In addition, she is the leader of a fierce band of warrior angels known as the Valkyries, whom on her or Odin's command choose whom shall die on the battlefield and be led to the golden halls of Valhalla.

So what is the woman's role in the modern Heathen Warrior religion I hear you cry! The answer is simple.....complete equality to that of the male warriors!

There is absolutely no reason why any woman cannot or should not follow the Warrior path; in fact I encourage it. My wife has an affinity with the Valkyrie. She even has one tattooed on her wrist and believe me she can cause havoc on any battlefield! So what are you waiting for? Get out there and start training!

In all seriousness though, we have to lead by example and show the non-Heathen world that we are a progressive folkish belief system free from any stigma that may tarnish other faiths. We must acknowledge that we are not perfect and that we make mistakes, that we are human after all and don't profess to have all the answers. We must stand tall and announce to the world that all are welcome and treated as equals as long as they mean us no harm. We must be proud of our ancestors and the soil we call home.

Marriage

"With a good woman, if you wish to enjoy

Her words and her good will,

Pledge her fairly and be faithful to it:

Enjoy the good you are given"

The Havamal

Every Heathen Warrior is only as good and as strong as the support and love that is supplied by his wife and/or soul mate. I truly believe that marriage is one of the greatest gifts we can ever receive and the hand of the person you love in that very special of ceremonies should be bordering on a semi-spiritual revelation. We as Warriors must embrace the union of these two lovers with open hearts regardless of sexual orientation. Everyone has the right to be happy and to be with the one they love.

The traditions and rituals of the Heathen hand fasting is a veritable minefield in today's chaotic and often confusing world regarding the Northern Traditions. So many organisations, groups, Hearths, and back room associations claim to have rites that are "The" correct and authentic hand-fasting rituals performed by the ancestors themselves and that all others are damn right wrong and should be ignored because there's is right! It is a sad state of affairs and it really gets to me when in-fighting between groups thwarts the growth of our indigenous religion. Unfortunately as history shows us, the Pagan community as a whole seems to get so far then destroys its own good hard work by engaging in jealous rivalry and self-imposing elitism. However, to be objective and unbiased I must state that a lot of these organisations are involved with other great work regarding our faith and its revival in today's modern world. I'm by no means stating that my ideas and philosophies are correct and that I have all the answers, but I feel it is time to expand and evolve our faith in a way that educates the world that in the most part has no idea regarding the real Heathen Warrior ethos.

That being said, I have to voice my opinion and say that for the most part I disagree with some of their views regarding rituals and wording. There are some historical records indicating some of the dialect and rituals used during the hand fasting but for the most part the records arc incomplete. Every group has made up what they believe to be the most perfect and accurate ritual, filling in the blanks with creative flair, each rite varying from others that are available to us. I have to point out that I am one of the growing number of Heathens who very much believe that you should research as much as you can from as many sources possible in advance of the big event. Search the internet, read as many books as you can and most importantly talk to other Heathens about how they organised theirs, then use what you like and enhance the ritual with words or actions you feel are appropriate. Naturally when talking to others you will be bombarded with ideas, some of which you will like, others you will dismiss out of hand; but remember it's your day and as long as you are happy and the pantheon and the ancestors are honoured, who's to tell you you're doing it wrong!

There are some traditions that I may suggest and I feel are deeply profound and convey a sense of spirituality that encompass the ideals of our faith. The most interesting and least known is incorporating a sword, set of keys and a Mjolnir (Thor's Hammer) with a large metal ring on top of it. It is believed that when a man and woman were performing the ceremony, the man would pass a set of keys through the ring of the hammer to the bride to signify her role in the home; then the bride would respond by passing a sword through the ring to the groom, symbolising his role as warrior and protector. Both would swear a vow upon the hammer, possibly due to the fact Thor is considered the God of the working man and of perseverance. I personally feel that this simple and humbling act speaks volumes about the love, responsibility and complete unity between the two lovers and signifies the lasting bond being created and swearing it together upon the hammer feels somewhat right in today's over the top, consumer-obsessed world where everyone wants a more lavish and expensive wedding than their neighbour. As far as I am concerned this ritual should be used more often, but that's just my personal opinion and won't be offended if you disagree!

Anyone with an ounce of common sense knows that any marriage has its share of ups and downs, trials and tribulations that if not tackled as united force can cause misery and upset and that it takes more than love alone to succeed. With hard work and tolerance we can, and we must always be prepared to compromise if we wish our marriage to succeed and stand the tests of time.

If we go ahead with the big day we must be aware of our responsibilities and the seriousness of the bond we are about to undertake. There are some things you must do out of respect, such as hailing the Gods and Goddesses, hailing our ancestors and creating a ritualized holy space, but all this information is available in other books and I am not an expert on such matters. I feel that it is not only necessary but polite to involve those that have paved the way for our faith, and of course hailing the High Ones needs no explanation.

Chapter Eight

The Natural Realm

"If you must journey to mountains and firths,

Take food and fodder with you"

The Havamal

When we take an objective and open-minded look at paganism as a whole it becomes obvious that a common trait exists that links each path together regardless of what "branch" of paganism we follow. I must point out that I am using the term Paganism as a general umbrella term that encompasses all the indigenous religions, but the "Elitists" and "Purists" out there may state they are completely different and have no links to other paths. I would have to disagree in one fundamental way. The common thread that unifies them is the fact that the natural world and all it encompasses takes centre stage in all aspects of the faith and is of paramount importance, not just in the ethical sense but when one is utilising magic and in ritual or for that matter, everyday life. Of course this is may seem quite obvious to us or anyone connected to any earth-based belief system, but a startling revelation to others less informed for whom paganism is still nothing but, "the Devil's work"!

For many years, the general consensus amongst the public at large has been that of humour towards earth-religions and has been, for the most part, a target for sniggering, ridicule and the brunt of many a hippy joke. Their limited attention span seems to stop once they have finished reading their stars in the daily paper! Then all they care about is what the latest star is wearing or spent a ridiculous sum of money on! However, despite all of these distractions it would appear that a renewed interest is being fuelled by the release of many a motion picture depicting "alternative" beliefs and a verity of pagan paths, tempting and urging people to explore their own ancestral and indigenous faiths. To my mind this in itself is a paradox. It both encourages me and saddens me in equal measure that it takes the silver screen or modern technology to motivate and galvanize people into action to re-establish links to our environmentally friendly Heathen past. It is apparent to me and others that as we as a race evolve and make huge leaps forward in both science and technology, we run the risk of straying further and further from the natural realm of which our ancestors gathered so much spiritual and emotional knowledge, but yet technology is drawing people's attention to the earth religions via movies, the internet and even social networking sites. So in the greater scheme of things, who am I to argue with the Gods and mess with their plan!

As hard as it seems sometimes (to me especially due to the fact I'm not a fan of technological reliance), we must evolve our faith and get with the times, allowing the belief system to push boundaries, for as we know it is organic and has a will of its own regardless of what you or I think! If technology is the environmental enemy then we must use its power for good. That being said, we must maintain our link to the natural realm and encourage our children and kin to do the same. To forget this bond could spell disaster for the future as a species.

The Energy that Flows

As Heathen Warriors we are acutely aware that there exists an inner energy, an Odinic force we Heathens call Ond that flows not just through us but everything around us. It is a force that links all the nine worlds of Yggdrasil. It has a cosmic ebb and flow of its own traversing time and space, travelling throughout the universe. Everything you can see, and for that matter all that you can't, possess this flow. The trees, living creatures, streams, mountains, rocks, wind and sky all possess this force. It is a tangible element that has the ability to be everywhere and nowhere at the same time.

This energy is not only the cornerstone of our inner strength but a living force that was crucial to our ancestors who relied heavily on the seasons for agriculture and trade. They believed it had its own motivations and emotions and that this energy had the power to feed or starve their people depending on the Gods' temperaments at that time or whether or not someone had upset them! Rearing cattle or growing crops all had to be meticulously planned if success was to be achieved; geographical and environmental knowledge was of paramount importance as was hard work and steadfastness. Utilising Shamanic magic our ancestors could "tap" into this energy, thus predicting and/or encouraging good harvests or warnings of dying crops. Their skill in reading the signs of the earth, those of the elements and even those up in the night sky were amazing, and for good reason. Failure was not an option when the whole tribe relied on self-sufficiency. Nowadays people are happy and secure in the fact that they can pop down to the shop for supplies, but for our ancestors no such conveniences or luxuries existed.

If this seems a little farfetched I would like to draw your attention to the fact that throughout history, even now in the present day and from all corners of the world there exist indigenous people utilising such energy, albeit by different names. From the Native American tribes to the Mongolian Nomads on the Russian Stepp, from the deserts of Africa to the Indo Pacific Rim all believe this energy exists and is directly and undoubtedly connected to the natural world and the Earth around them. They see themselves, and quite rightly so, as nothing more than lodgers being allowed to live where they do and as such recognise the fact that they have certain ethical and spiritual responsibilities towards the land. The cardinal rule faced by such peoples was and still is the unwavering belief that when living off the land you must not be greedy and take more than is necessary. If you take something, you have a moral duty and must give something back in return. If you take firewood, you plant a tree or at least give respect. If you kill an animal you honour its bravery. This not only creates a spiritual and emotionally dependant bond with the environment, Gods and the energy itself, but a mutually beneficial symbiotic bond that can last indefinitely as long as the tribe doesn't over step the mark and forget their environmental ethics. I personally find this a fascinating subject and emotionally uplifting when I think that even now in today's capitalistic world indigenous people still live by the laws set down by their ancestors and hold true their beliefs. I am truly humbled and feel that these people need the protection of their respective governments and urge others to get involved to safeguard their way of life; for you never know when such safeguards will be needed for you and I.

I must admit to me and my fellow warriors there is nothing better than going off into the woods and having a small fire and enjoying the great outdoors amongst good company. We do this for two reasons: for rituals and for fun. Unfortunately this country is so incredibly small compared to mainland Europe and is very densely populated thus affecting the amount of places you or I can go and enjoy such pursuits. In the areas where we can go and visit the wilderness, we are inevitably faced with the fact that we are not allowed to have open fires and even campsites are restrictive these days. I have to say that our country seems to be a little draconian regarding its camping laws. I'm undecided whether this is due to the fact that the minority have spoiled it for the majority or that our government are just out of touch with nature, but when we compare these laws to those of Norway we start to feel a little depressed! I myself have spent time in Norway and find it to be a fantastic country. There, the law states you can camp anywhere as long as it is a certain distance from a dwelling. It would appear no one takes advantage of this law and acts in a responsible way towards the woods and nature itself. I personally feel this is a fantastic quality and tradition passed down from their ancestors and feel a little embarrassed that we in England don't follow suit.

There is however some remaining places we can visit and camp without too many restrictions. I urge everyone to visit the northwest highlands of Scotland and even the islands off the west coast - fantastic scenery and open space galore. It truly nourishes the soul when faced with such rugged beauty, ancient forests and cavernous lochs, not to mention the feeling of putting your own little life into perspective. One truly needs to be out in the thick of the great outdoors to feel the sense of over powering awe these landscapes possess; it really does connect you to the Ond energy that flows all around us. My wife and I used to camp on a very isolated beach overlooking the Atlantic on the Isle of Lewis. Breath-taking isn't the word. This place holds a very special place in our hearts and always will, but please don't ask me where it is; it's top secret! May I suggest you go out and explore for yourself, take some close friends and find that special place that talks to you. We all need a place of spiritual tranquillity far from the hustle and bustle of modern living. Of course there are other places we can visit like the many national parks scattered across the country and of course there is Snowdonia situated in the north of Wales. Wherever you go, I urge you that if you do have a fire in the woods please be respectful and act responsibly and leave no trace of you being there; take your litter home and leave as you find. This is not just common sense but essential.

I think it's clear that we must all do our bit when it comes to recycling and helping the planet cope with the rubbish we as a species produce. I have to admit that I am quite naive and clueless when it comes to recycling and get confused with all the mixed messages given out by government agencies not to mention the green activists. I realise that I am somewhat lacking in this department and feel it is my duty to learn more and urge everyone to do the same.

We are all painfully aware, regardless of what faith we follow that the earth's resources are drying up and something needs to be done in the present to safeguard the future. I, as do many others, believe this is a universal crisis that transcends religion or race. As Heathen Warriors we accept the responsibility that comes with sharing this planet and are not afraid to get stuck in when we can and to at least try to make a difference. Sometimes we might feel that we are fighting a losing battle, for the corridors of power seem to side with and protect the large corporations who are repeatedly raping our planet in the name of a fast buck. When faced with such insurmountable odds, we must look to the Noble Virtues and our inner fortitude. We must unite and stand against such tyranny and corruption and stand our ground whilst shouting, "We will not give up!" and "You will listen to us!", before it's too late. Regardless of how much we do, no matter how insignificant it seems, it helps take our faith, family and kin in the right direction.

One person can make a difference if they shout loud enough.

Animals

I am often asked what my views are regarding the hunting of animals, be it for sport or for food and the answer may surprise you. As a Heathen Warrior I believe that any animal has the same rights to life as you or I. The same energy flows in all beings regardless of species and to my mind they have just as much claim to this planet as we do. However there are some exceptional circumstances that we need to clarify whilst talking about this subject.

We as Heathen Warriors deplore any cruelty to animals in the name of sport or fun and hold any who engage in such activities in complete contempt. There is absolutely no need to hunt and kill just for the sake of killing or to prove what great hunters we are. That being said, if we are ever attacked by an animal we feel we are completely justified to defend ourselves and more often than not this leads to the animal being killed. I would like to state that if this happens I feel it is only right to honour the animal and its spirit and utilize the remains be it by the eating of its meat or the use of its body or fur for clothing or other tasks. Our ancestors were completely aware of this fact and would not let anything go to waste, so why should we? They also believed that by consuming the animal's flesh the spirit and attributes of that animal would be endowed to them and the wearing of the animal's fur would give them super natural powers assisting them in either battle or food hunting.(I will explore this further in a later chapter.) To keep this reverent tradition alive, I think it's imperative that we should also educate our young that meat does not just appear in the supermarket via some teleportation device but show them where their food is really coming from, thereby allowing the tradition to continue into the future.

When all is said and done, we as Heathen Warriors feel it is absolutely justified to kill an animal if we intend to eat it. I accept the vegetarian view as well as the vegans' standpoint but believe it is vital that meat be a part of our balanced day to day diet. Some argue that in this day and age we have no need to kill animals for food and that there are alternatives, but in my opinion mankind has always eaten meat and there has always been a food chain and always will be. Some may think me provocative and politically incorrect in my views but in today's world where untested genetically modified "food" is being thrust upon us I believe we should all grow, raise and slaughter our own food as much as possible, not just because it brings us closer to nature but for the simple fact that we know exactly where it has come from.

I myself have three furry pets. I have a cat named Mia, a kitten named Gimli and a rather dopey Rottweiler called Duke. I love these animals and can't imagine life without them even if they do drive me crazy at times. You may be wondering why I am mentioning my pets and the answer is simple. Having domestic pets not only keeps and maintains a connection to the animal kingdom but also teaches us discipline. We must always remember that these animals rely on us for their survival and in return give unconditional love and loyalty. This type of loyalty is in itself a type of therapy and has been proven to work wonders with those of us that have ever felt a bit down in the dumps. Some of you may think, "Oh my god he's got a Rottweiler, they are demon dogs!" but this couldn't be further from the truth. Any animal has the capacity to be aggressive and there is no denying that some idiotic people in society teach this breed to be a guard dog, but this is not necessary as the dog already has a built in defence mode and will protect the owners without hesitation or command. As a warrior we have to utilise any tool we have at our disposal. I am not suggesting we use the dog as a weapon but rather as an early warning system to alert us to possible danger (I know for a fact no one gets into my garden without alerting my Duke!). Whilst on this subject it may be of interest to you that the Roman army never used dogs as sentries to protect their camps at night; they actually used geese, due to the fact that nothing gets past them without whipping them up into frenzy! An extremely clever tactic, I think.

Chapter Nine

Heathen Magic and Spiritual Defence

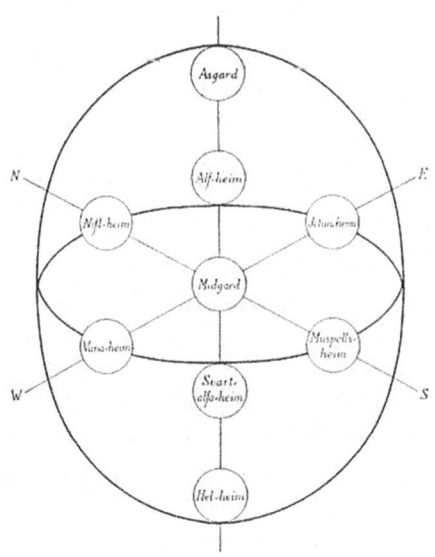

"They gave me no bread,

They gave me no mead,

I looked down;

with a loud cry

I took up runes;

from that tree I fell."

The Havamal

The word "magic" is subjective. Everyone has their own interpretation of what magic is and how it can be used, or for that matter, if it really exists at all. There are those that will defend their own magical system and condone others. There will be those who deem all magic as nothing more than the psychological meanderings of the mentally unstable or those who express an interest but are afraid to explore due to negative press for fear of ridicule from their closest friends and family. I think that we would all agree that if our ancestors were to visit us in today's world, they would be astonished and marvel at our technology and no doubt view it as a form of magic or possibly as a divine gift from the Gods. So on that basis would it not be correct to view anything we don't know or understand as a form of magic? Is magic just a name given to that of which we have no explanation? Is the seed of imagination that formulates into an idea a form of magic in itself? If so, where do the seeds of magic come from and can we use them for a more spiritual and emotional cause in the world of the Heathen Warrior?

For the most part, the populace at large are content to leave magic in the world of Harry Potter and feel it has no place in the "real" world; however there seems to be a resurgence of interest in magical systems around the globe. One only has to visit the new age section in any good bookstore or a specialist shop to find a startling array of books dealing with the esoteric and occult magical systems from all faiths and belief systems. It can range from Tarot reading to Witchcraft and Wicca, from High Ritualistic Magic to Voodoo, to name but a few. So if magic does not exist, why are so many books available to us? Why are there more and more people from all walks of life spending their hard-earned money on fairy tales? The more sceptical among you would state that authors are cashing in on the magic-crazed Harry Potter generation in a hope to make a fast buck, and to a certain degree I would have to agree with this analysis, but surely not everybody is doing it just for the money, are they? There must be some validation of magical workings amid the barrage of literary nonsense; they can't all be charlatans and nonsensical lunatics running around the fringes of esoteric belief systems.

But this literary magical phenomena is nothing new. Throughout history there have been many books of magic written by faiths that you may not have directly associated with magic, for example the Buddhists' Tibetan Book of the Dead or even the Jewish Kabala. These books were said to contain incredible magical power and were revered and treated with the upmost respect. However, once again the "free speech" police stick their oars in! Some mainstream religions deem all magical workings or faiths as the work of the devil and anybody dabbling with such arts is in league with the devil himself! What they fail to grasp is that even the Bible contains magic; their magical manifestations go by the name "miracles", so by definition their argument is inherently flawed, as they too must be in cahoots with the horny red one!

As Heathen Warriors most of us are completely at ease with the basis of magic and the place it holds within our culture. There are many examples when the warrior is used within magical circles and is not just confined to Heathen practices. I personally know of a very good friend of mine who is often asked to walk the boundaries of a circle to protect and ward off bad intent. He himself is Heathen and follows the warrior path but has done this task for Wiccan circles and Druidic gatherings. He has told me he sees it as a duty regardless of the faith involved and if asked is happy to lend his Warrior energy to those who seek his assistance. I myself have never partaken in such boundary-walking rituals but completely understand and support my friend's decision to do so. However, some may decide that we do not need to study, practice or advocate the magical side of our faith and are content with the ritualistic aspect of our belief system. In my opinion this blinds us to the exploration of our inner selves and the energy around us, thus weakening our spirit in this realm and all others. There for I would personally urge all Heathen Warriors to at least explore the magical side of our faith for it is interwoven with our ancestor's martial art skills; only then can we make an informed choice based on a balanced personal experience. One must also remember that magic comes in many guises and at first glance are not as mundane as they first appear, as we will see later.

First though we shall delve deeper into the options open to us and discover that there are many forms of magic that can aid us in our endeavours and gift us knowledge and power regarding our warrior path. In all these magical workings we can utilise the knowledge gained to heal us or even obtain intelligence concerning our enemies or our life in general. They can protect us as well as cause harm to others and sometimes may even incur a fee or penalty depending on the form of magic used and what God or Goddess we seek help from. I should point out that these disciplines are incredibly powerful and should not be undertaken frivolously. One should be aware that journeying to the other realms to gain knowledge is not a game, can be very dangerous and should always be treated as such.

Even though there are many paths to choose from, you don't have to choose just one and stick to it. I myself engage in most of the disciplines and use what is important for my specific goal. I have used more than one in a single ritual to obtain the answer I require so there is no hard and fast rule governing what you can and cannot use. You must find your own balance and locate what works for you regardless of what others may tell you.

I will however pass on some things I have learned from my own personal experiences when dealing with magic and spiritual defence and give tips that I find useful when conducting rituals. At first glance you may think that defending yourself in the "real" world is completely different from protection in the "other" realms, but you would be mistaken. The same game plan can be utilised in both arenas. As with any attack against your person or towards a loved one (and surmising you cannot avoid said action) you have three courses of action.

Deflection

This option is using minimal personal energy or magical force to deflect the attack away from you, causing no harm to the attacker and keeping you out of harm's way.

Disruption

Option two is using equal force to manoeuvre and lead the attack into a position in which you have the advantage and to which the assailant has no knowledge until the action has taken place. It is both subtle and has a psychological effect once the attacker realises what has happened. The end result is no harm being done to yourself but some kind of harm being done to the assailant, but nothing too damaging.

Destruction

The final choice is one that has a devastating effect. This choice is using more force than is directed at you to instantly stop and "destroy" the attack before any harm is sustained. I have to point out that this will most certainly end with the attacker receiving extreme damage either physically or spiritually, so one's conscious must be clear that you had no other choice.

Below is a list of some of the magical paths, disciplines and skills available to the Heathen Warrior for us to learn and experiment with. As this is not a book specifically on Heathen Magic I shall be brief in my descriptions. If you find a topic to your liking and feel you wish to explore it more, may I suggest that you purchase a book dealing with the magical path that pangs your interest. I will also incorporate some exercises or ideas for you to try, to act as a starting block for your magical journey.

Rune Risting

The drawing or carving of Runes to power a spell or incantation. Each rune has a specific magical meaning and can be used singularly for a specific purpose. However they can be combined to create a bind rune. This unites the power of each rune. This type of magical working can be found through the Sagas and Eddas and is still used today in Iceland within the Icelandic sorcery traditions. They were traditionally drawn on wood or carved into leather. Through the ages they have been used for everyday things like good harvest or favourable weather but also used in the extreme, such as wishing harm on an enemy.

▪ Try some basic rune carving and creating a simple talisman for a wanted task. Start off small then progress at a steady pace until you have the knowledge to expand your ritual work. As you progress and learn more about each rune start to formulate your own bind runes.

Rune Divination

Using the whole runic alphabet (futhark) for the purpose of divination. There are many ways to read them in this capacity. The most common is the three runes, past present and future configuration. Can assist with all manner of questions and is viewed as a direct "hotline" to the Gods and Goddesses. This practice is still used in modern times and is the most commonly seen in esoteric circles. However, there are those who claim to be "rune masters" and "experts" in the runes. Please do not be fooled by such claims as there is no such thing as a rune master and never was, even during our ancestors' era. Even Odin never claimed to be a master and was continually learning and honing his skills regarding the runes.

- Start by learning each rune individually. Learn their attributes in the positive sense as well as the negative (reversed). Make notes of all things appertaining to each rune, including Gods and Goddesses. Spend one week (or however long you feel is necessary) on each rune and try to absorb the essence of it; don't be too eager to move onto the next one. Carry the rune around with you wherever you go in a pouch or bag, maybe even wear it as part of a necklace or other item of jewellery.

Runic Galdr

The chanting of rune names to empower magical spells. This can be done to hypnotic drumbeats. Different beats represent different elements and are of varying speeds, thus affecting the rhythm of the ritual. I personally use this in conjunction with the Shamanic Seidr. I have heard of some folk who only sing specific runes for the purpose intended but others repeat the whole Futhark; at the end of the day it is personal preference to which you use. I personally swap and change my mind depending on the ritual.

▪ Learn the runes individually and sing one each week until you have found the true frequency that you believe belongs to that particular rune. Try different pitches. I personally find low range pitches work for me. I also find going out into the wilderness helps me focus the energy and does not make me feel self-conscious singing at the top of my voice, unless of course you have a fantastic singing voice; in which case go for it at top volume in your house!

Galdr

The use of song, poems and chants to empower spells and incantations. Some use long poems or songs, others use short direct sentences repeated over and over again. Galdr as opposed to Runic Galdr puts the emphasis on longer verse and not just the rune names.

▪ As with Rune Galdr I tend to go out into the wilds to focus on the signing and to achieve powerful energy. Choose your favourite poem and sing it or if you prefer create your own homage to the High Ones and practice that. Repetition is the key when utilising Galdr. Once again it is the intent behind the words and as such, work better if they are your own and from the heart. The words might have come to you via some other shamanic workings, thus could be a gift from the High Ones themselves. You just never know.

Seidr

The Shamanic form of Heathen magic said to be associated with the Goddess Frejya. Traditionally used by women but there are some records of men engaging in this practice. It is used to travel between the nine worlds in a trance-like state, more often than not done to drum beats. Can be done alone but myself and my kin prefer to work in a group when conducting Seidr as this lends more energy to the ritual. However, there are times when a personal matter needs to be addressed on your own, where you don't have to divulge the nature of the ritual to others and can be safe from possible ridicule and forced opinions.

▪ There are some things that we should bear in mind when engaging in Seidr, elements you may not have thought of. When I work alone I take in to consideration the location of the ritual. I have an affinity with the Earth and the dwarfs, so I tend to look for caves, hollows and such like thus making contact and travelling easier. I also like using forests and secluded spots by a flowing river to add vital energy to the proceedings. Depending "where" you wish to travel should denote the location of the ritual; never underestimate the power of your surroundings when planning your trip. One should also contemplate temperature. Extreme heat or cold can affect the human body and aid the travelling experience; many cultures around the world use these natural elements to assist their ritualistic wonderings. Please bear in mind though that it can be dangerous and if using extreme temperatures should always be part of a group, thus help is at hand should anything go wrong.

Wortcraft

The use of herbs and flowers as magical charms or hand made into incense. These can be burned when conducting ritual or other magical workings. I personally have no experience regarding handmade items in this art but am eager to learn more! However, it is common practice that when entering ritual the sense of smell can relax and help you enter the travelling state, thus the use of shop purchased incense or joss sticks. Not all of us have the time or skill to produce our own range of smells for personal use. That being said my wife has made her own unique incense for ritual work based around the Goddess Frejya and I have to say it smells fantastic! I'm sure our Lady of the Swans loves the aroma that emanates from our house when it's lit!

▪ Explore the things each God or Goddess likes; investigate the flowers and herbs associated to them. Meditate to see if they send you any messages regarding the smells they enjoy. Is it fruity, pungent or subtle? Is the incense going to be honey-based? My opinion is that they should all have the base ingredient of honey due to the fact that we all know the High Ones love mead! I personally carve runes into candles and use them as a visual aid to focus my ritual work. This can be used within all aspects of Heathen magic as it also includes the scent from the candle itself.

Rammankin

The art of obtaining and utilising superhuman strength within the martial arts.

▪ Of course this can be put down to rigorous training, and one's own personal will to excel at our chosen martial art. Determination and fortitude can help us attain a level of superhuman skill that to others may appear "magical", but then again, who is to say it isn't? How often do we look at record-breaking athletes and marvel at their "superhuman" skills? Convinced that they must be "on something" to achieve the accolades they have obtained? Magic or sheer personal will power? Or maybe a little of both? It's all a matter of subjective opinion.

Shapeshifting

Within the Heathen faith there are many examples of shape-shifting, ranging from the berserker warriors changing into bears on the field of battle to Loki beguiling his foes and even Odin himself changing into animals or even females to attain some goal! I have my own interpretations of this art that I will go into in more detail later.

▪ Use the Helm of Awe (shown later) as a conduit regarding shape-shifting. For more information see further in this chapter.

Ofreskir

The art of second sight, those who can obtain information from the spirit world. There are many sources of volva (priestesses) communicating with the spirit world for the purpose of obtaining information, a skill still practiced today in some Heathen circles. I myself know those very adept at this particular skill.

▪ I believe that meditation is the key to this skill and must be used in conjunction with Seidr. We must travel to the other realms to obtain the information we require. Again, we can use other tricks from all paths of Heathen magic to assist us in obtaining this skill.

As we can see there are many different magical paths open to us within the Heathen faith, each with its own purpose and each leading us on a journey of discovery like no other. I would say though that despite their differences there are some common factors that, in my opinion, have to be taken into consideration no matter which path you follow. For my money, location, seasonal timing, audio and visual stimuli and specific smells are of paramount importance. Take time in planning your magical workings but above all listen to your instinct when formulating a plan of attack, I have read a lot of books and talked to a lot of people who say that things should be done "at this time" or that "you are wrong" if you question the timing of their magical workings. I am a firm believer that magic is as personal and as unique as you and I and as such must approach it from an individualistic, instinctual perspective, our own personal will and direct energy force differs for all of us, thus it makes no sense that a specific and rigid way will work universally. As a footnote I tend to be minimalistic with items used within my magical workings. I don't for one minute subscribe to the notion that you need loads of bells and whistles, wands and robes, statues and figurines and a host of other "tat" to conduct a worthwhile experience. My base rule is: keep it primitive, keep it simple and keep it direct. You may not agree, but each to their own. If you feel the need to do the opposite of what I have suggested then go for it, after all, this is just my opinion.

Animal Magic and the Martial Arts

Bronze plate found at Oland, Sweden depicting Berserker.

I doubt there are many people reading this that have not heard, at one time or another, the term Berserker. The Berserker were said to be among the elite of the Norse fighting machine, the Nordic Special Forces, the warriors closest to Odin and was extremely distinguishable from others on the battlefield. Their fighting style was said to be based on the "Bear Strength" and reputedly used magical abilities to shape-shift and confuse their enemies. It is said that their initiations were a closely guarded secret and that very few people ever witnessed them first hand. However, some scholars have found evidence to suggest that when an initiate wished to gain entry to the Berserker clan he had to first run into a cave where a bear skin had been thrown and retrieve it, along with the claw of the resident bear! It is also said that they had a form of ritualistic dance that was performed by moonlight; however I can find little evidence to support such claims. That being said, going by other warrior cults and their practices it wouldn't surprise me and feel it is highly plausible. It is also said that when not engaging in battle the Berserker would often wander around the countryside challenging people to holmgang to earn a living - this was picking fights for money! Within our traditions there existed other formidable fighting units that were used for specific jobs and all had their own unique skill set and characteristics. The Ulfhendnar, for example, were famous for wearing wolf skins covering chain mail whose main weapon of choice was a spear, but unlike like the Berserkers did not enter battle in small squads but rather entered combat single-handedly, utilising guerrilla tactics. There are the Ulfhamir who also adorned themselves with wolf skins but unlike the Berserkers did not utilise any armour. These groups of fighting men had an affinity to the wolf and the qualities it represents. When summoned, the warrior became one with the animal in a magical state. There seems to have been a specific cult that worshipped the wolf but finding hard evidence is proving elusive. There is some conjecture amongst historical scholars that they were incredibly secretive regarding their rituals and practices, bordering on secret society status, while others suggest they were killed off due to the changing attitudes towards warfare and the power they wielded. This was in some respects akin to the fate the Knights Templar encountered in mainland Europe some years later. It has also been said and suggested that their main allegiance was to that of Odin the Allfather for he was and is the God of magic and shape-shifting; this of course would make perfect sense regarding the attributes these clansmen were said to possess.

There also existed a group of warriors loosely known as the Boar cult. These supercharged warriors adapted the small unit strategy of the Svinfylking or the "Boar's Head" formation, were said to possess super human strength and were reputedly incredibly bloodthirsty. They were also reputed to be masters of disguise and extremely adept with escape and evasion tactics, possessing an intimate knowledge regarding the terrain around them as well as bush craft and wilderness survival techniques. It has been suggested that these warriors would be the first warriors into battle, predominantly to break enemy lines, and once they had completed their mission were immediately followed by other shock troops. Some military historians have cited the fact that on the face of it, this boar's head formation is good at first but leaves your sides unguarded, allowing the enemy to flank you, hence the use of quick movements followed by other troops like the Berserkers and wolf cult warriors.

Superb tactics and uncanny acts of warfare were not just reserved for the Viking hordes; others from our Heathen past demonstrate the same grasp of scare tactics and tactical awareness. The Harii (Latinized German for "Warriors") for example painted their shields and their whole bodies black and used to attack only on the darkest nights, thus giving the impression of a ghostly non-human fighting force. It is said by historians at the time that the night would fill with their bloodcurdling screams as they rushed to attack, a tactic I find fascinating considering they were around during the first century A.D and scared the daylights out of the invading Roman army. At that point in history, the Roman army was the finest, most organised and well-funded military force in the world but lacked the unconventional warfare skills needed to stop a guerrilla military unit fuelled by northern magic and the utter desperation to save their indigenous homeland. Some believe they are the basis of the Fallen Warrior Einherjar of Norse mythology hundreds of years later but others question such a theory. Either way it never fails to impress me that with cunning and tactical adaptability they managed to enrage and disrupt the Roman army, a far superiorly trained fighting force. It just goes to show that a small group of "unconventional" warriors can make a difference regardless of the size of force pitted against them and strike fear into an enemy who not only believes his own hype but who seriously underestimates his foe!

So how did they gain their fearsome reputation? The Berserkers and other animal-based units were said to don the skins of animals and enter the battle in a self-imposed rage with or without armour and sometimes even naked, thus allowing them to fight without regard for their own safety and having a psychological advantage over the enemy. They were said to be near unstoppable and there are many archaeological references of the Berserker and his ilk in action from all around the globe. Some scholars think the Berserkers specifically, entered the rage state by way of drugged food alone but my theory is multi-layered. Yes, I believe that some sort of drug or alcohol was introduced but I also believe that the animal skins they wore gave them a link to the power and strength of the animal used, thus putting them in a mind-set of primal savagery. If we combine these elements with a magical trance summoned by way of shamanic Galdr or Seidr and focusing the power or energy we call Ond we can see that it makes for a highly unstable and fearless warrior capable of immense damage and acts of heroism depending which side you were on! Whether you believe that shamanic magic had a direct spiritual bearing on their state of mind or whether the fury was just the will of the warrior's individual bloodlust it is without doubt a factor our ancestors believed in, and based on my own experiences I believe this also. I myself have taken part in shamanic trance rituals and have felt the intense rush of freedom and exhilaration that comes with summoning the power of the bear or the wolf or any other animal for that matter. The act of summoning the animal spirit, focusing our Hamingla (Ond used in a personal sense) can transform and heighten our awareness and abilities thus forging a link to our primitive warrior soul as well as our ancestors' past. So readers beware; don't take this magic lightly or for that matter leave an axe nearby when conducting said ritual!

The Gods and Goddesses

As we have mentioned before there are many Gods and Goddesses we can call upon for guidance and assistance depending on our specific dilemma or problem. As Heathen Warriors I feel it is important to know what deities possess the knowledge, skill and desire for battle regardless of the type of fight we face, and approach them accordingly. I have decided to list a few of the deities that are, in my opinion, the ones who can aid and protect us as a whole. Please be aware that this is by no means a definitive list and once again I urge you to explore for yourself.

During your Warrior journey it may become apparent that a specific deity jumps out at you, and you may find yourself forming a bond with a particular God or Goddess that endures and possibly over shadows the decision to choose. Don't feel you are being detrimental to others if you work with this one in isolation. I myself have a bond with Ullr; not only am I a winter person but I have an interest and skill with a bow, qualities all associated with Ullr the God of the winter hunt. When making contact all I ask is that you research and approach your chosen deity with respect. Be aware of the flowers or gifts they like, choose your words and offerings diligently and always be true of heart and honest with your intentions.

THOR

Probably the most famous of all the Heathen gods, Thor is the God of thunder, sky and fertility. He is the son of Odin and hailed as the protector of Asgard and Midgard, a formidable warrior possessing great attributes and skills. His weapon of choice is his mighty magical hammer Mojinir. Many view Thor as the God of the working man and as such wear a pendant of his magical hammer around their necks as a talisman to protect them. I myself wear such a pendant. Easy to speak to and always ready to help, he is said to be good natured and enjoys his drink!

ODIN

Alongside Thor, Odin is probably the most recognisable of the Norse pantheon of deities. He is the ruler of the Gods and the Nine Worlds. He is known as the father of battle and is the God of poetry and death. His weapons of choice are his magical spear Gungnir, general magical abilities and his intelligence. He is said to wander amongst his subjects disguised as a beggar to keep watch on the affairs of mortal men. He is intelligent, quick witted and very knowledgeable regarding magic and the Runes. He is also known as "The Allfather". Take care when contacting Odin, as he is very powerful and doesn't suffer fools gladly.

TYR

Tyr is known as the God of single combat, justice and war. He is a ferocious warrior and his weapon of choice is his sword. He is the son of Odin and the poster boy for the heroic ideal within the Northern Traditions. He lost his hand during a game of wits with the wolf Fenriz whilst trying to bind him. He is reputedly quick tempered but fair and is regarded as the god of spiritual discipline. The rune Tiwaz is associated with Tyr and is often worn as a talisman for protection. This rune is extremely powerful when used in Heathen magic.

FREYJA

Freyja is a Goddess associated with beauty, fertility, war, death and seidr magic. She is a formidable warrior and her weapons of choice are a spear and shield. She also wears a cloak of falcon feathers that gives her invisibility - a handy trick for a Heathen Warrior! She is often referred to as a shield maiden and is the leader of the warrior women known as the Valkyries whose job it is to take the heroic slain from the field of battle to Valhalla. She is both beautiful and wise and never backs down from a fight. She definitely gives the men a run for their money! My wife has an affinity with Freyja and even has a Valkyrie tattooed on her wrist.

ULLR

Ullr is the step son of Thor and is associated with the winter months. His weapon of choice is his Bow and is looked upon as the God of hunting, trapping, bush craft skills, skiing and archery. He is also known for his combat skills in all its forms, especially single combat. Not a vast amount is known but scholars suggest he has been worshipped in one form or another for a longer period than first thought, possibly pre-dating the Vikings themselves. He is still popular in the extreme Northern Hemisphere and amongst the outdoor pursuits fraternity.

FORSETI

Forseti is a little known God but a worthy consort in times of trouble. He is the Norse God of justice and especially court justice and law. He is said to be of quiet demeanour but extremely intelligent and diligent. He is the ruler of Glitnir, a shining realm where all legal disputes are settled. I'm unaware what his weapon of choice is but feel it could do some damage if he threw one of his law books at you!

SKADI

Skadi is the Goddess associated with the winter months and of the great hunt. She is valiant, brave and a skilled warrior. She is viewed as the Goddess of justice, vengeance and righteous anger. Like Ullr, her weapon of choice is the bow.

EIR

The Goddess Eir is one of the handmaidens of Freyja. She is considered a Goddess of healing, which could come in handy. I have had no direct dealings with her personally but have heard she will only engage and teach women the arts of healing and meditation but there's no harm in trying!

123

THE EINHERJAR

This is a slightly different and unconventional one. The Einherjar are in fact our dead ancestors who died bravely on the battlefield then were taken by the Valkyries to Valhalla. As we involve ourselves with Heathen magic and our rituals we automatically ask our ancestors to join us and welcome them to our hearth and circle whenever we participate. However I see no harm in asking them directly and specifically for their assistance as opposed to asking a deity.

Runes, Talismans and Protection

It is a fact that every faith has its own symbol, a focal point and visual aid to link the human existence to their own personal divine force as well as for protection and comfort in times of distress. Within the Northern Tradition there exists a multitude of symbols to choose from depending on what motivates you, the things you have an affinity to, your own character and the deity to which you have an affiliation. They can be as complicated, intricate or as plain as you see fit. As I stated before I have a connection with Ullr but currently wear a Thor's hammer around my neck. This may seem a little confusing to you, but to me it feels completely natural. You have to make your own choice with regards to visual acknowledgement of our faith and must not be swayed by others and their opinions. Popular protective amulets amongst Heathens are:

THE SUN WHEEL, ALSO KNOWN AS THE EYE OF ODIN Fig. 1

This represents the overall power of the Allfather. An ancient and world symbol and one of the most widely used by followers of the Northern Tradition, it also can represent the solar calendar. Many cultures around the world use this symbol or a variation of it. It is also used by the Native Americans who call it The Medicine Wheel.

THE TRIPLE HORN Fig. 2

This is used as a sign of devotion to the Northern Tradition as a whole as well as Odin, and also can represent the love of mead and brotherhood within the Northern Tradition. It is also believed that the interlocking nature of the symbol represents the intricate weave of the lore and philosophies within the Northern Traditions. I personally believe that the continuous forward motion of the sharp ends represents the faith ever moving forward and evolving.

<u>THE VALKNUT</u> Fig. 3

This depicts Odin's power over death and represents the slain. It is also known as the knot of the slain. Its nine points represent the nine worlds within the Norse cosmology, of which Odin is the chief God. It has been seen on many graves. Not recommended as a tattoo as it gives Odin free reign to take you as he sees fit, regardless if you want to go or not.

<u>GUNGNIR</u> Fig. 4

A runic amulet charged with and representing Odin's magical spear. It is said to be invulnerable. It was forged by the dwarves and is said it never misses its target. I and others I know use this symbol for focus and to throw our energy into a specific target or goal that has to be achieved.

<u>SLEIPNIR</u> Fig. 5

Odin's eight-legged horse on which he rides into battle and across the night sky during the wild hunt. Represents speed, stamina and courage. Interestingly, the lore behind the steed is that the God Loki shape-shifted into a mare and conceived Sleipnir as a gift to Odin.

<u>MJOLNIR OR THOR'S HAMMER</u> Fig. 6

Representing the magical weapon used by Thor. Used for protection and strength in the face of adversity. It is an incredible powerful talisman to wear and is seen as the amulet for the everyday working man. This is possibly one of the most widely recognised symbols worn by Heathens and those within our faith; however it is also used by the far right and should never be associated with the resurgence of Nazism. It is not a hate symbol but part of our Heathen heritage

IRMINSUL

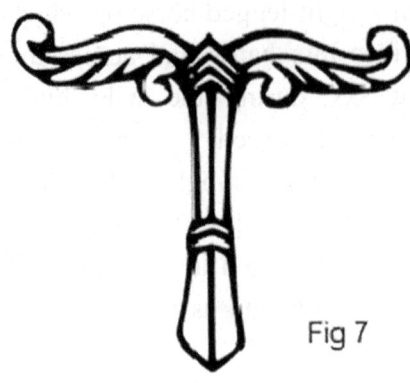

Meaning mighty pillar in Anglo Saxon, it is used as a symbol of unity between man and the cosmos, possibly relating to the god Tyr due to the resemblance to the Tiwaz rune. Within the Norse cosmology it is referred to as Yggdrasil, the world tree and is the tree that connects all the nine worlds together. To travel to another realm one must follow the branches to your destination.

Fig 7

EINHERJAR Fig. 8

A depiction of the valiant warriors slain and taken to Valhalla by the Valkyrie, a tribute to ancestors and the Warrior ideal within the Northern Tradition. In my opinion this symbol not only pleases the High Ones but also connects us to those who have forged the way before us and is also a testament to those who will follow in our footsteps. Not all Heathens will agree with me regarding the use of this symbol but I truly believe that it honours our ancestors and we should never forget their sacrifices.

TROLL CROSS Fig. 9

A symbol made of iron worn to ward off Trolls, Dark Elves and evil spirits, always a good choice when travelling the lower worlds. Possibly based on the Odal rune, however it's hard to find any concrete evidence regarding the history of the Troll Cross. I would wear or use this symbol when travelling into the lower worlds via Seidr due to the fact that I tend to use caves and you never know what's lurking about in the dark!

That being said the most simple amulets worn by Heathens are based on runes, be it a singular one or an amalgamation of more than one, known as a bind rune. This blending of two runes unites and magnifies the magical power output of the talisman by each rune complementing the other; however, one must always be careful when creating such powerful objects and must do extensive research regarding each rune and its meaning. The last thing you want is for the runes to cancel each other out, leaving the talisman ineffective and thereby useless. As you may have already guessed, the runes are incredibly secretive and deceptively coy regarding their power and influence appertaining to magical workings and knowledge. It takes time, skill and extreme patience to extract the information we desire from them. They are not toys and once you start to delve below the surface, become mind boggling tools for assistance and guidance as we walk the long Heathen Warrior road of life.

Each rune has a link to a specific God or Goddess and it is personal choice which one we wear. However as each rune has a meaning in itself we can still wear it without the allegiance to the deity to which it is associated.

Icelandic Staves and the Power of Words

There is a long standing and fascinating shamanic tradition in Iceland that has to be mentioned when we discuss Heathen magic and the use within the Warrior aspect, both orally and in the written format. For centuries sorcerers have weaved and recorded a fantastic rune-based magical system utilising Staves and pictorial spells that I personally have a great interest in and have every desire to explore further in the future. Even into the early 20th century the native Icelanders still engaged heavily in its practices and unlike the rest of the Northern Hemisphere kept a fantastic record of the rituals and practices their ancestors used in everyday life. The book itself is known as The Galdrabok or Icelandic Grimoire, and contains not only magical staves for protection and attack but invocations to Christian deities, necromancy and rituals for the Northern Gods and Goddesses. Ironically a lot of the shamanic staves were adapted, utilised and even advocated by the Christian monks during the 16th and 17th centuries, possibly due to the sway the old ways still had over most of the Icelandic population even after Christianisation. Regardless of the monks' motivations, the written works are indeed a thing of wonder, have an other-worldly feel about them and at some level feel primeval and primitive yet powerful and invoking. They are at this time locked securely away in an Icelandic museum's vault. Even today the Icelandic people are famed the world over for their literary prowess and have more authors per capita than any other country in the world. So it stands to reason when discussing words and their power we look to the extreme north for clarification and assistance. Before we examine the Staves and their magical ability, let's take a brief look at words themselves and the role they can play in Heathen magic and the Warrior path.

Words are indeed powerful whether spoken aloud or in written form and should never be underestimated. They have the power to convey our intent, emotion and inner power thus generating a response that suits our own personal will and desire at that specific moment in time. Every word has the power to create an emotional vibration and response to anyone who listens. If I say the word "hate", for example, with vehemence and complete sincerity over and over again it creates a wake that emanates to whoever it is aimed. You can physically feel the word and the meaning behind it. By this definition we can utilise words to create magical shields to protect ourselves or a weapon to assist us on our Warrior path and in times of need. I often used this form of Heathen magic when working on nightclub doors. When dealing with a violent confrontation I was always relaxed and calm but when an attack was imminent I suddenly, and to the individual completely out of the blue, used a combination of words, body language and reverse psychology to immediately disarm and confuse the would-be attacker, thus defusing the situation and keeping the assailant on the back foot. Nine times out of ten they would walk away utterly confused and unsure to what just took place, their will to fight evaporated. It may seem farfetched but a single word has the power to stop a man in his tracks if it is said with complete conviction and has our personal will and Ond behind it. It doesn't just need to be used in a violent situation; it can be used passively too in any situation we see fit. Try it for yourself and see what happens!

Staves and Bindrunes

For all intents and purposes, staves are Icelandic Heathen magical symbols drawn on leather, stone or parchment, tailor-made for a specific spell or incantation. Like the runes, they can be as complicated or as simple as the user sees fit, depending of course on the reason we are implementing them. We as Heathen Warriors are privileged to have a vast array of staves available to us, immortalized in archaeological records for use as talismans or for use in our own shamanic rituals and magical workings. I find it fascinating that even in today's modern world Icelandic wrestlers still use staves drawn on paper and placed in their shoes to aid victory in forthcoming bouts, a testament to the enduring folkish belief system even after all these years of Christian rule. Even though it is not an exhaustive list, I have endeavoured to list below some staves and bind runes that I believe can be beneficial to us on our Warrior path. As I have said before, this is just the tip of the iceberg when it comes to Heathen magic and what I have presented is a snippet of how we as warriors can utilise our ancestors' knowledge in our day to day lives. Of course we must bear in mind that our ancestors had specific problems and developed magical workings to combat such threats and trials accordingly. Some of these may have no bearing on our lives in today's world so as with everything it is down to the individual to use what is useful and discard what they feel is irrelevant. I do, however, feel we should at least learn and explore our shamanic past so that, at the very least, we can admire our ancestors' contribution to the esoteric. But of course this is just my opinion!

Helm of Awe

Fig. 1a

To induce fear in an enemy, to defend against the abuse of power. I feel this is THE one to use and rate this one the best for our purpose travelling the Warrior path. It has been speculated that it can also be used in the magical art of Seidr and is predominantly used with illusory magic, to help escape or to disguise. The arrows on the arms denote which way the energy is flowing. Facing out, you are sending the energy from your body as a shield or as a weapon. Facing in towards the centre denotes pulling all the magical force from nature inwardly for use in either ritual or summoning strength. A very powerful symbol to aid shape-shifting. Simply draw the symbol on the ground and conduct your ritual on top, making sure of course that the arrows are facing in towards the centre. I personally feel it should be during the cold winter months that the shape-shifting ritual take place. I feel the primitive animalistic feel to the colder months gives extra weight to our goal and makes it easier to tap into the "beast". Of course this works for me but feel free to experiment and find your own way.

Ottastfur

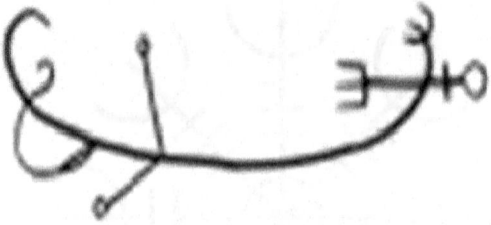

Fig. 2a

An Icelandic symbol for inducing fear and confusion in the enemy, a very handy tool for the Heathen Warrior in both this world and for use magically.

Gapaldur and Ginfaxi

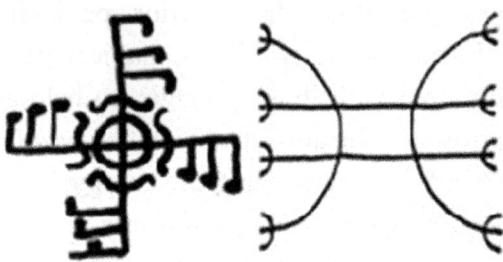

Fig. 3a and 3b

One to be placed in each shoe to ensure victory in Icelandic wrestling. Can also be used in any form of single combat. I would also say that it could be used in any team sport.

Hreathigaldur

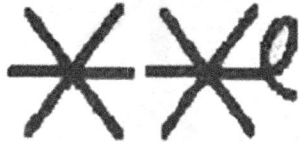

Fig. 4a

Puts fear and uncertainty in the enemy. No other explanation needed.

End Strife

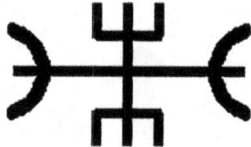

Fig. 5a

Good Luck Bind Rune

Fig. 6a

Good Health Bind Rune

Fig. 7a

Win Lawsuit Bind Rune

Fig. 8a

<u>Healing Bind Rune</u>

Fig. 9a

<u>Tyr Rune</u>

Fig. 10a

Ullr Rune

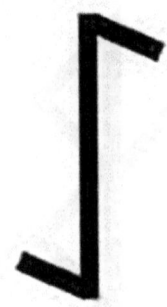

Fig. 11a

Vegvisir

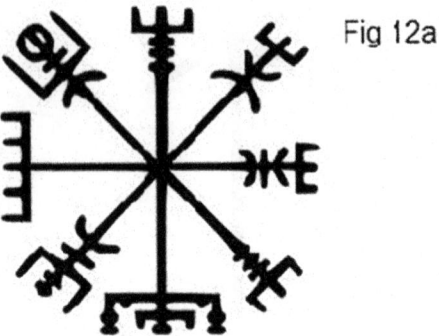

Fig 12a

Runic compass to prevent from getting lost, a variation of the helm of awe but with a more nautical twist.

Svefnthorn

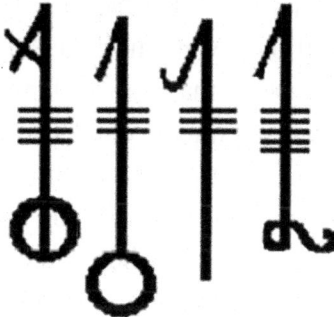

Fig. 13 a

For a restful sleep. After a hard day's fighting every warrior needs to get some proper sleep!

Lasabrojotur

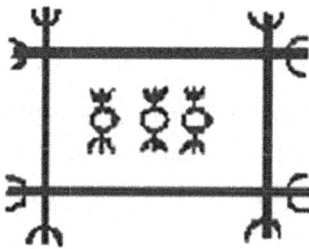

Fig. 14 a

To escape bindings or pick locks. This could be very handy if you are in a bit of a pickle!

The Metaphorical Shield

To conclude this chapter, I feel it is important to discuss and explain what I call the "Metaphorical Shield". At face value it may not appear to be a magical tool and may even seem completely out of place within the context of this chapter, but I feel it is a skill that is extremely useful for us as Heathen Warriors be it on the spiritual level or here in the earthly realm. The techniques can be used when engaging in shamanic travelling or for use when facing confrontations or specific problems in our day to day lives. I believe that our ancestors would have known the attributes of the metaphorical shield and would have used it as a common sense tool when dealing with others.

I, like many others in today's society have chosen to adorn my body with extensive tattoo artwork (both arms are completely covered as well as other parts of my body) and body jewellery, and therefore give off the impression to some that I am nothing more than an uneducated thug who spends his time running around beating up small animals whilst mugging old ladies for their pension! Even though I am big built, sporting a rather fetching and manly beard and look like a bad-ass biker, this image couldn't be further from the truth! Yes, I can handle myself, yes, I don't suffer fools gladly and yes, I do look somewhat menacing but don't make the mistake that you know what I'm really like just because of the way I look and the stereotypical image I portray. Therein lies the irony, doesn't it? I, like most of humanity, have the private, behind-closed-doors "real" me and the image I choose to show others outside my immediate circle and kin. Ninety percent of the time I want people to look at me and think to themselves, "Flipping heck! He looks mean; I think I'll leave him alone!", because in today's predatory society, bullies and those with no moral compass prey on those that appear weaker than themselves and I for one don't intend to be a target. As Heathen Warriors, I feel it is our duty to give off an air of strength, and even if we are shaking with fear inside, give the impression that we are not fazed under the circumstances presented. We have to be strong for our families, loved ones, kin and faith and stand tall, hold our ground and not turn and flee, just as our ancestors stood their ground all those years ago. Anyone who states they are never afraid is in my opinion lying, regardless of how big and mean they look. Even the mightiest warrior has had his courage tested.

At the human level, the image we show others is our metaphorical shield, a deliberate ploy to either appear weak when we are strong or vice versa, a sneaky protective tactic to insulate ourselves from any harm that others may intend for us or to dissuade others from a course of action not to our liking. With this self-created image we can be anything we desire; we can stand out from a crowed or blend in and disappear when needed. Considering this, wouldn't it be safe to say that this psychological and tactical tool is a kind of modern day shape-shifting? If we flit from one version of ourselves to the other are we not changing our mannerisms, the way we stand, talk or even our whole personality? To me, this is a form of shape-shifting martial art! Some have used this skill to devastating effect. Have you ever wondered how people lose their life savings to a rather convincing confidence trickster? You wouldn't have fallen for that trick, you tell yourself. Would you? What you have to understand is that these people are experts at shape-shifting, creating other versions of themselves that appear completely plausible and legitimate, thus fooling those around them and luring their target into a false sense of security. Another example could be the police officer; do you trust him just because he is in a uniform? Could he be one of those officers who is corrupt and abuses his power at any given opportunity? Is the officer automatically the good guy and the biker he is arguing with the bad guy?

When we really take time to examine the role in which the individual psychological attitude and personal perception can assist us, not only on the battlefield but in our everyday lives we can see that it can be used as a protective shield, thereby giving you the ability to throw your enemy off guard, a distinct advantage in any endeavour undertaken. If you can create an alternative persona detached from the real you it acts as a buffer thus helping to control your fear: the fear of possible injury or the fear of failure. It is a known fact that over the years intelligence agencies from around the world have utilised these psy-ops techniques with impressive results. Of course these skills can be used to downplay aggression and encourage co-operation as opposed to attack. The term "hearts and minds" is an obvious example. This trick particularly is used by the confidence trickster or on a bigger scale by countries for use in political subversion and governmental destabilization. I am of the opinion that the Heathen Warrior needs to be aware, thus able to adapt these tricks and incorporate them into his /her spiritual and martial training. We need the ability to fight those who seek to do us harm and protect those we love no matter what form of attack is before us.

The point of this topic is to let you know that if others find merit in these skills and can utilise these tactics then so can you. You have the ability to adapt and flow with your surroundings and must use it to your advantage when travelling the Warrior path. As hard as it is, try not to judge by appearances alone. Look, listen and trust your instinct, always be on your guard and never take anyone at face value. I urge everyone to explore or at least arm yourself with the knowledge that others may use these skills against you. Good luck and happy shape-shifting.

Chapter Ten

Orlog, Wyrd and Sacred Oaths

"To ask well, to answer rightly,

Are the marks of a wise man:

Men must speak of men's deeds,

What happens may not be hidden"

The Havamal

As we humbly stumble down the path of the Heathen Warrior and explore the faith and ethical foundations our ancestors courageously laid down for us, we may start to become blasé and may even begin to assume on face value that it is a somewhat forthright and uncomplicated religion, marvelling at our own capacity for absorbing all it has to offer.

Just as we think we have cracked it and think we fully understand the spiritual, emotional, magical and physical dynamics, the truth becomes all too clear. We have only scratched the surface! For as we delve deeper into the world of the Heathen belief system and specifically the Warrior aspect within it, we will at some point undoubtedly and with absolute certainty find ourselves up against subjects and/or theories that either contradict or confuse us to the point of sitting there scratching our heads in complete bewilderment wondering where it all went wrong! Don't be too hard on yourself should you reach this point. It stands to reason that different people will find different topics confusing, depending on their individual intellectual prowess, common sense or capacity for exploring new "radical" and "far out" theories. It is inevitable that at some point we will all reach a point of treading spiritual water whilst walking our path of discovery. I myself fell foul to such a hurdle and when asked what my own personal conceptual challenge was I would have to say that in my opinion the most misunderstood of Heathen concepts and a veritable minefield of various opinions is that of Orlog and Wyrd and how they relate to us as Heathen Warriors and the world around us.

As these topics are so incredibly intertwined and multi-layered I shall try to explain in simple English the reasoning behind each and why there is so much confusion and opposed views regarding the roles or even if they are the same "force" by all but a different name. Please bear with me as I blunder my way through a maze of contradictions and hope you get the general gist of my ramblings!

ORLOG

At base level Orlog is seen by Heathens as the base law, fundamental to all things around us including the scientific laws of gravity, physics and cosmology. One can even say it is the force behind the concept of cause and effect. On the personal level it is believed to be what governs everything moralistic and as it is neutral can be both beneficial and detrimental depending on the actions we take and the choices we make. We may think we have planned for every possible contingency but other forces dictate otherwise. Wow, no wonder people find it an intellectual stumbling block! There are some that also attribute Orlog to a form of destiny in its rawest form.

Even though some may disagree, I am a firm believer that Orlog is a supreme force flowing through our lives and makes itself known regardless whether we believe in it or not. To our ancestors their belief in Orlog was such that if a person committed a crime (of any description) that was deemed unworthy or not honourable in the eyes of the folk, their shame would be inherently passed to their kin and so on until a descendant did an act deemed worthy to remove such stigma caused by their relative. For all intense and purposes their debt to karma would be cleared and their Orlog repaired, thus starting from square one again. If, however, the said offender did not repair their relatives' Orlog, they would be ostracized and would have no social standing within the tribe or have the ability to cast any sort of vote regarding the affairs of the collective. Obviously our ancestors felt that as Warriors it was crucial to keep on the right side of Orlog, for when in battle you wanted and needed to have complete faith in the warrior stood next to you and at a spiritual level didn't want his or hers bad Orlog to rub off on you!

WYRD

Now this is where it can get a little confusing. Wyrd is your destiny already written regardless of whether you believe in it or not. Our ancestors believed that your fate was already written a very long time ago and was pre-determined through space and time even before you existed, and regardless of what you did you couldn't change the fact that certain things were going to happen! At first glance they appear to be the same thing but let me give you some scenarios that may help you to gain a better understanding of this topic.

Scenario One

Orlog - You plan to take a trip with your wife. You have planned your route and prepared your car for the journey. You have done all the right things like checking the oil and fuel, etc. You check the map once again. Even though there are four different route choices you have used your free will to choose this specific one and feel confident with your decision. You have based your decision on the fact that Orlog states the roads exists even though you are at home and are not physically on them at the time of your choice.

Wyrd - You and your wife leave your house and follow your own directions to your destination, but when you're halfway there, you realise that the road is closed for repairs and you have to take a diversion down a narrow country lane. Whilst travelling down the country lane your tyre gets a puncture and you have to pull over to fix it, none of which you planned.

Even though you used your free will to choose what route to take and your Orlog denoted that the roads would be there, your Wyrd had other plans and placed pre-determined problems before you that you could never have anticipated. You have the ability to choose what road to take but have no control over events that present themselves whilst on your journey. All you can do is adapt to challenges that present themselves and try to move forward to your original goal with the least amount of discord.

Scenario Two

Wyrd - You are at a bar with some friends. You had no intention of going out that night but decided at the last minute that you would and made the decision on a whim. A few hours into your night you notice a rather large-set man staring at you and talking to his friends. You realise that he is going to start trouble and you decide to leave. As you do you are confronted by the thug who starts a verbal tirade and punches you in the face. Wyrd pre-planned this event even though it seems like bad luck and no amount of side-stepping was going to change it. Of course you may have done something to warrant such a reaction and feel to blame and are willing to accept the conflict. Then again you may feel that you are blameless and feel guilty and stupid for not acting sooner and start thinking that if you had only done this or that the trouble could have been avoided.

Orlog - You now have the free will choice to act as you see fit. You can use Orlog in any way you deem right. Do you fight back or run away? Either way the choice is yours but your actions may have far-reaching consequences for you and your loved ones. If you fight you may lose and get beaten up. If you win the man may find out where you live and come looking for you with a group of his friends, thus putting your family in danger. You may get arrested and receive a criminal record, thus possibly affecting your job. The course of action you take is also confined to your personality traits, social conditioning and level of fear regarding physical confrontation, as well as the reaction to those around you, all of which has a bearing on the final outcome of this situation.

As you can see the ramifications are endless and it is impossible to second guess what is probable or predict any given outcome regardless of what information you think you have. Another thought would be if I stood at a crossroads, it is my choice to take any of the turnings and may feel destiny has no sway over my decision. I may choose left or I may choose right; who's to say? I make my decision and continue to walk. But who's to say that Wyrd hadn't known that and it was already a foregone conclusion regardless of the personal belief that I actually had a choice? We as warriors must be aware that any decision made has consequences and that making rash decisions can have a possible detrimental effect on our spiritual, emotional and physical being and when all is said and done we must come to terms with the fact that we can't fight fate. We must all face death no matter how it presents itself but at least we can choose how we face it, either with fear or true of heart and with courage and dignity.

As we have seen the relationship between these two topics is at best confusing and can surely be a bone of contention when discussing with others the merits of each and the effects on those around us, let alone the actual specific description of what they are. Each person has the right to explain as they see fit and what one would grasp another may find completely nonsensical; again, it is all about the personal approach and level of understanding. It would be folly to suggest that I have all the answers and fully comprehend myself the relationships they have. I certainly would never say I am an authority on such meaningful meanderings, or that mine is the definitive explanation of Wyrd and Orlog. View my contribution as an added footnote to the hundreds of other descriptions available for you to read on the internet. When all is said and done, I have tried to be honest and open and feel I have explained it as concisely as possible and hope you at least get the vague understanding of the role each plays within the warrior ethos.

OATHS

As warriors it is of paramount importance that we lead by example. Our very actions and reasonings must be beyond repute and we must never stray from the core values that govern our faith and family unit. We are the spear-end of the Heathen movement and must be good will ambassadors of our faith as well as its protectors. Only by "doing" rather than "saying" can we encourage and energise those who look up to us to follow in our footsteps and help keep our indigenous belief system thriving in modern times. We must be a pillar of moral virtue and try to remain objective in whatever endeavour we undertake. Of course this may seem like common sense but I think you will agree with me when I say that it can be hard to stick to the winding path of pure intent in this crazy world of ours. To keep things under control when those around us are having a meltdown can be incredibly taxing. Our fortitude must be resolute but can we really guarantee we will not falter? When faced with stark choices can we trust ourselves to make the right one when others depend on us? That's why I feel we need this folkish belief system and family unit to ground us, to make sure we have a suitable framework and support structure to help us in times of trouble, be it spiritual, or economical. But be aware that no man is an island and we have to rely on those closest to us and know for sure that they will be there in dire times not just when it suits them or when times are plentiful. But how can we truly believe them when they say they will be there for us or that they will be true to their word when it all goes pear-shaped?

In all walks of life there will be people who say one thing, promise the earth but when the chips are down would drop you like a hot potato. That is why as Heathens we must make sure we surround ourselves with those that we can trust wholeheartedly, whatever fate throws at us. We must be one hundred percent certain that our brothers and sisters will back us whenever we need them; but do we just take them at their word or is there a more concrete and unbreakable vow that forever binds you before the Gods and Goddesses? The answer is "yes" and that most sacred of bonds is our Oath.

To every Heathen an Oath is an unbreakable vow made before our pantheon and in front of our peers and fellow Heathens. It is of huge importance and should never be taken lightly or frivolously and the seriousness should never be underestimated. It is not merely just an "I promise to....", but a spiritual and emotional bond forged before our ancestors and the glue that keeps the fabric of our society together. The oath is absolute sacrosanct and is the holiest of holies within the Heathen traditions.

Our ancestors realised at an early stage that trade and commerce was a necessity for survival and that due to the lack of a written language and the long distances between traders a bond or promise was needed that could be used as a contract between men that could not be broken under fear of death. It was completely legal to kill someone who broke an oath if witnesses were available and our peers believed it to be justifiable. Of course in today's world that just isn't plausible and against the law of the land regardless of what country we reside in (specifically referring to the Western world and Northern Hemisphere). It still doesn't detract from the seriousness of the Oath taken and the impact of said oath-breaking to ourselves and our immediate kin. When your livelihood and the welfare of your family is at stake, an oath between you and a business partner is an incredibly important and binding affair. As we have talked about before, the word honour is paramount within our tradition and it is our duty to act honourable in all our dealings regardless whether it is in business or our everyday lives. It therefore must be an unbreakable virtue and our oath must be worth something, not just within our community but also when dealing with others outside of our folk. It is this forthright and honourable promise that educates those who are sceptical regarding the Heathen movement and its belief practices.

As Heathen Warriors our main oath focus would be that to our fellow warriors and that of our leader or king. Of course unless we are soldiers in a modern army we do not have a direct king or queen to swear alliance to like our ancestors did, so in my opinion it would be an oath sworn to our warrior brothers and to our Gods and Goddesses that would hold sway in our lives (unwavering loyalty and allegiance to our families is of course inherent within our belief system). As with Heathen Warrior tradition, I believe that we men and women following this path must own a weapon be it sword, axe, spear or knife that can be of dual purpose and practical. It can act as our personal weapon and that of our official oath-swearing tool that all our oaths are sworn upon. However it is accepted that in these modern times some of us have separate items that work in isolation regarding practical tools and a specific swearing weapon. It can be as plain or as intricate as you see fit and should have a great deal of meaning to the individual warrior. I myself own a sword for just said oath-swearing purposes but also have my own practical weapon of choice. Fellow Heathen Warriors I know have everything ranging from a sacred spear to a handmade Thor's hammer that is staggering in its detail and beauty and took over a year to make! As with most things we have discussed it is personal choice in what shape our oath-swearing implement may take; however in my opinion it should be a weapon of some description hallowed and sanctified before our Gods and Goddesses. Since we are walking the warrior's path and all it stands for within our traditions it seems only right and appropriate.

The final thought I would ask you to bear in mind regarding oaths is to remember that we as Heathens are only as good as our word. If we fall short and make such a promise on a whim and without fully comprehending the ramifications of breaking it we only serve as a weak link within our religion and folk collective. Others from the outside will have their fears confirmed that the modern world is no such place for our ancestral beliefs and that they have every right to view us with suspicion and doubts regarding our motivations and aspirations for the future. We must always strive for the moral high ground and show the outside world that Heathen Warriors are not mindless thugs, but honourable men and women folk who prize loyalty and honesty above all else. We must also be aware that if we were to go back on our oaths we may very well fall out of favour with our Gods and Goddesses who we seek guidance from and that could affect not only ourselves but future generations of our kin.

Chapter Eleven

Ancestors in a Modern Age

"Wise is he not who is never silent,

Mouthing meaningless words:

A glib tongue that goes on chattering

Sings to its own harm"

The Havamal

Whether we are amateur historians, scholarly academics, casual social observers or for that matter just slightly curious none of us can fail to notice that regardless of the time span separating us, we in the modern age share a lot of characteristics and social traits, not to mention values and seasonal celebrations to those of our ancestors. On the face of it does not matter from what geo-specific peoples we feel we originate from or what ancestral home we call our own, the main point is as long as it comes from the Northern

Hemisphere and is related to the Northern Traditions with regard to original beliefs and religious practices, be it Anglo-Saxon, Viking, Dane etc., we can utilise historically accounts and records to compare past and present societies for the purpose of historically and modern day clarification. Of course once we start to investigate, there are a lot of things we still have or use that are directly linked to our ancestors and their way of life. One only has to look at the obvious examples first, like our laws and judicial system or our very language itself, not to mention our democratic basis for our political governing. Then we delve deeper into the realms of the not so obvious. Our days of the week, for example, are named after Norse Gods and Goddesses. The traditional Christmas tree has nothing to do with Christianity but is a Norse Pagan tradition and the tinsel you decorate your tree with was originally believed to be the entrails of an enemy! Brightly coloured tree baubles were originally called Witch balls; Easter is Pagan, as is Halloween. There are too many examples to mention in this book and can be easily researched on the internet. Back in modern times, as we watch closely and really observe the actions of those around us, we can't help but compare our own personal actions and traditions to those of our ancestors. When all is said and done, all we have to do to get an idea of how our ancestors lived is take a close look at current social trends, even though attitudes towards them may have wavered somewhat, therefore giving us the possibility to glimpse days gone by and the effects of said actions within our folk and society at large. This begs two million-dollar questions: are we really that different from our ancestors and what characteristics do we still possess?

Let us firstly look at the Warrior-specific influence on today's society and try to dissect the reasoning behind it and whether it still holds any sway over us in a technological obsessed world.

It is common knowledge that every Friday and Saturday night, pubs and clubs across the country and in every city and town around the U.K are inundated with those who wish to eat, drink and be merry. It has also become a sad fact that many a town and city centre has become an incredibly scary and dangerous place to be after dark, thus forcing some law abiding citizens to stay away rather than fall victim to predatory villains and those of a morally dubious nature. It is also a known fact that once all the inhibitions are gone and the banter has stopped, the animalistic territorial instinct takes over and after so much alcohol has been consumed the inevitable posturing and fighting begins, not just causing antisocial behaviour and extreme levels of violence but giving our emergency services a rather eventful and busy night. Some may ask the question regarding why our country has a history of senseless fighting and binge drinking then make the sweeping statement, "You don't see other countries acting like that!" Of course it would be easy to dismiss these actions as the minority causing turmoil for the rest of the populace, but I personally believe it stems back to our ancestors and is more to do with our tribal past then anyone wants to give credit. Thus to understand our modern actions we must once again look to our ancestors for the answers.

When trying to find the answers we seek we must first look at the social structure and the impact the warrior aspect had within the tribal homestead and village. It is obvious that as we in the modern era have the public house as a social hub within our community our ancestors must have had their equivalent. The main focal point for our ancestors and the tribal unit was the mead hall or long house. This main structure was central to all

Heathens and served as meeting hall, pub and council chambers and was available to all within the social unit. Our ancestors utilised it for entertaining, storytelling and for a wide variety of social events, hence it became an incredible important and spiritual place for everyone, including the Warriors within the tribe. (You don't have to be a genius to figure out where I'm going with this and to realise what the links are to our Heathen past.) Upon entering there would be blessings and news followed by the inevitable feasting and drinking. The warriors of course were in attendance and were undoubtedly wowing their kin with tales of high seas adventures. The air would be jovial and the alcohol flowed freely, the atmosphere full of laughter and friendly bantering between brothers and kin. As time moved on and amidst the smoky hall the festivities were indulged in by all, but inevitably with so many talented warriors concentrated in one place and the alcohol pouring like a waterfall there was bound to be conflict of egos or challenges being offered to ascertain who was the most fearsome warrior or other such meaningful questions. Fighting was then a foregone conclusion to settle such disputes. To us this may seem rather barbaric but one has to realise that even though there was fighting on a regular basis and the mead hall presented itself as a rather rough place, it was not only seen as a rite of passage but was considered normal within the warrior aspect and an integral part of being a man and a Heathen Warrior. No one bared any grudge and it was immediately forgotten after the fray, thus becoming brothers again. It was seen as a test between kin, friendly bonding within the warrior cult and essential training for future battles. The psychological effect was also incredibly important and served as a training aid to the warriors. If bested by another within your band, it forced you to assess your own shortcomings and personal weaknesses and ask very personal and illuminating questions about yourself, thus pushing you to train harder and raise the bar of your martial skill. The war band only had room for what they considered to be the warrior elite and the weak were encouraged to become stronger. If they failed to do this they were no longer a part of the warrior cult or sent back to the beginning to start their warrior training all over again, depending of course on how lenient the commander was. One also has to bear in mind that our ancestors' fighting styles and military tactics were based on animals that were abundant in their homelands, be it the wolf, bear or boar. As in the wild, the alpha male would nip the younger, less experienced one to not only exert dominance but to bring them up to speed with the skills they needed to survive not just on their own but as a family unit. This is no different to modern military units who break a recruit down before building him/her into a soldier worthy of the regiment cap badge. This is necessary to build a bond between those who stand beside them in peace time and on the battlefield.

As we can see, the basis for our modern drinking and fighting culture appears to stem back to the days our ancestors spent within the mead hall having a scrap whilst consuming vast amounts of mead! As a result, I believe this culture has, over centuries, become woven directly into the very fabric of our social consciousness. However I am of the opinion that over the years the "larger lout" generations have forgotten the reasoning behind such bonding and truly lost sight of the benefits it originally intended to teach. It has evolved into recklessly and non-directional fighting with others for the sake of ego alone and those who fight are not brothers in arms but view each other as enemies, those who pose a possible threat to each other's own masculinity. They have become like wild beasts and in the midst of alcohol-fuelled invincibility feel they are the alpha male, but unbeknown to them are fighting for nothing other than a sense of self-worth obscured by the lack of self-discipline and sense of honour. Without the sense of brotherhood and the spiritual aspect found within our ancestral teachings and the emotional ties that unites them they become nothing but barbarians in the truest sense of the world. Nowadays such behaviour is illegal and is deemed socially unacceptable and I have to agree with this due to the moronic reasoning behind the violent conflict itself. However, I and many other Heathen Warriors are mature enough to realise that it is, in part, due to our genetic makeup and that all men regardless of faith have the primal savage warrior/hunter energy within us. Some can use it whenever we see fit whilst others need some kind of catalyst or substance to utilise its power.

I also feel it is partly geographical .As an island we have always had to fight off invaders since time began and that others have always wanted to exploit our nation's natural resources, thus, cementing the warrior aspect within our social mind-set. It stands to reason that if a people are constantly at war or under the threat of war, the social framework of that culture ultimately ends up revolving around the premise of war and the attributes surrounding the survival of conflict. Please be aware that I am not condoning the "weekend warrior" culture and I hold anyone who indulges in such stupidity without good reason in complete contempt, and find them to be uneducated fools. However, I do have an understanding of where the primitive warrior energy comes from and feel once people understand the reasoning and origins behind such historical and spiritual energy and admit to themselves that it is inherent within us all as a folkish people we can as a nation focus such energy and embrace the warrior ethos thus bringing us closer to our ancestors and unifying our faith. Please do not misunderstand my meaning so I shall spell it out loud and clear for those of you who fail to grasp my musings and the context of their meanings. We as Heathen Warriors have absolutely NO wish to live in a militarised world or any sort of dictatorship, far from it. Freedom for all is of paramount importance regardless of what some Heathen groups state and that the TRUE Heathen Warrior will stand tall and fight those who try and subjugate those weaker than them due to either greed or twisted ideology. I wish to point out the undeniable fact, as many of my folk will agree to, that once you truly understand something (regardless of what it is and what context it is used) and comprehend all the mechanics that make it work, you can harness its power and control it, thus avoiding and defusing any negativity associated with it or its use. To me and my kin this is common sense. Again, I shall use the analogy of fire. It is neutral in its existence. It is neither good nor evil but can be used for either depending on the individual's will and intent of the person using it. If this is the case then I draw the conclusion that ANY form of energy, be it physical or spiritual, and if used wisely of course and with good intent can be beneficial to us as Warriors, not just in the battles we face but in our everyday lives. That can only be a good thing, but there are more things we share with our tribal past that lends credence to this theory.

Another example of ancestors in our modern age is the mob mentality and the theory that when all together the individual's own feelings and moral compass takes a back seat and becomes a bystander as they give in to the flowing of energy around them, thus indulging in acts they may never have contemplated if they had been on their own. I believe that within this mob the will of a few has the ability to manipulate the energy, thus blinding others to socially unacceptable acts going on around them. Today thousands flock to see the sports stars go head to head and our favourite team play that crucial game regardless of what sport it is. We, as human beings, need the feeling of belonging to a group, a group that shares ideals and the same motivations, a place we can feel safe and united with other of the same ilk. For our ancestors this was built on the Warrior cult and the attributes surrounding it. Nowadays sport has replaced this and has become a focal point for family and kin for both relaxation and spending family time with loved ones, not forgetting the feeling of self-worth that comes with healthy competition. For all its good points there are elements that damage the unity of said social gatherings. The inevitable conflict between opposing teams, for example, blights many a sporting event forcing the nonviolent folk to one side or possibly putting them in harm's way. Of course this I believe is another aspect of our primitive warrior culture coming through and has replaced the honour bound traditions with the "excuse" for latent violence. If we look at football hooligans, for example, this trend started in the U.K and then spread around the world like a virus. Every weekend groups of men would meet up for the sole purpose of fighting for no other reason but for the name of their team. I dislike football and the violence that these men take part in, but, to some degree I understand why they do it. In today's nanny state the warrior heart of men has been suppressed and we have become soft; the image of masculinity has been downplayed and the roles of each gender blurred. This has eventually led to us to be programmed into dismissing our primal energy. I'm not suggesting that we should regress and devolve into sexist Neanderthals or anything as idiotic like that, but we must be free to remember who we are and celebrate that side of our ancestral nature. The result of masculine suppression is the uncontrollable reawakening for any excuse presented, thus directing the energy in a completely unfocused way creating violence for the sake of violence. To those who take part it is seen as some "fun" but I am of the opinion that there are deeper psychological reasons lying hidden beneath the surface and that these reasons are directly linked to our ancestors, whether we have desire to admit it or not. Even if you are not in agreement with me it certainly falls into the category of food for thought.

At the risk of sounding somewhat dramatic I feel that I have to point out some issues relating to the warrior aspect that need to be addressed. In my opinion, within the modern Pagan world there has been too much emphasis placed on the female Goddess aspect of the earth religions, thus letting the male aspect fall by the wayside. I am not for one second suggesting that we don't need the Goddess element, far from it! Regardless of the path followed it is imperative that we strike a balance, but we must include or at least acknowledge the masculine primal energy and must actively avoid completely dismissing its relevance and the balance needed between both genders, whether it is magically and/or ritually. As Heathen Warriors I feel we must fly the flag for the male role within the status quo of indigenous belief systems. For anyone with an ounce of intelligence it is common sense that we need both male and female; for one without the other is useless. The father figure is just as important as the mother and I feel we must celebrate masculinity and the attributes associated with it. It is not my intention to tell you how to incorporate it into your faith but feel it is imperative that it is used in equal measure and is not something that is seen as surplus to requirements.

Heathen Celebrations

As with all religions there are days that we as Heathens celebrate and indulge with in the form of feasting, drinking and being with those of similar mindset and our loved ones. I have to say that in this modern world sometimes it isn't practical due to work commitments or other such distractions but we should also make an effort to the best of our abilities and at least try to make these days special. I myself work strange shift patterns and sometimes don't have the means or free time to take part on specific days. I have to admit sometimes feel I am disrespecting those on high by not taking time off work but then take solace in the fact that the Gods and Goddesses realise my circumstances and don't hold it against me; for as we all know ours is the religion of the working man and the High Ones know I am out providing for my family! That being said, I encourage all Heathen Warriors to make time for our celebrations and to give thanks to our pantheon for all their wisdom and bounty they bestow upon us, even if we are a few days out. To the purists my ideas may seem like a complete travesty and unthinkable but once again due to the age we live in we have to rethink and adapt to current social and economic circumstances. One has to bear in mind that our ancestors were all of the same religion. Therefore, when it came to religious festivals the whole community took time out to take part and enjoy the festivities, each doing their bit to make the day or night run smoothly and thereby giving themselves a role to play and the feeling of self-worth before the Gods and Goddesses. Unfortunately we have to face the stark truth that in the modern world our faith is not a recognised religion in the U.K. (It is in other countries and there is a movement within the U.K. to promote and get Heathenism recognised as such and I for one applaud the work such groups are doing.) So we have no special rights regarding religious holidays (unlike other non-indigenous belief systems) and if we work in a job where our holidays are planned out in advance (as are mine to the tune of five years!) and cannot book time off when we want, then we are literally up the creek without a paddle! Therefore we have to do the best we can and I make no apologies for it; I answer only to the Gods!

I have decided to list some of the dates we Heathens consider special and urge all Heathen Warriors to celebrate them. As usual this is not a definitive list and your own research is important.

Yuletide

19th – 26th December

One of the main Heathen celebrations, Yuletide has existed long before Christianity. A time for feasting and drinking with kin and family, it also incorporates the winter solstice. Food and drink should be plentiful and hospitality should always be encouraged.

Ostara

19th – 26th March

The festival of springtime, rebirth, and awakening from winter's slumber, it also includes the spring equinox.

Wulpurgisnight

30th April – 1st May

A day of celebrating the Goddess Frejya and all her attributes and is often celebrated with bonfires.

Midsummer Blot

21st – 26th June

Celebrations revolve around growth and bounty for our folk; it also incorporates the summer solstice.

Haustblot (Autumn's Blessing)

19th – 26th September

A celebration of the autumn and the autumn equinox.

Winter's Night (Winter's Blessing)

31st October – 1st November

Heathen New Year, and a time when family is to be together with feasting and drinking. I personally love this time of year due to my link with Ullr, the God of the winter months.

Ancestors' Day (Einherjar Day)

11th November

Also known as Remembrance Sunday, a day when we remember those who have given their lives and made sacrifices for our country and faith and celebrate our ancestors. As a Heathen Warrior, I feel this day is incredibly important because without them we would all be living in a very different world.

Clothing and the Ritual Attire Debate

There are some individual Heathens and groups out there that feel that to be truly immersed and faithful to the Northern Tradition we all have to be doing exactly the same things and that there is no room for negotiations. In their eyes this is the only way to follow the path and that all other ideas are sacrilege and should be discouraged. Of course this is ludicrous. These purists are trying to dominate any free thought, thus suppressing the one thing that makes our faith great: the ability to grow and evolve. However, I have to state that they are for the most part referring to the absolute belief that everything has to be done bang on time or that we have to dress in the clothes our ancestors wore when conducting rituals and other sacred celebrations. When tackling the subject of ritual attire I have to say that in my opinion this is a tricky subject and presents us with a double-edged sword. Whilst I don't agree with all their views, I am of the opinion that any ritual should be sacrosanct and should not only be serious but an enjoyable affair regardless of what faith you follow. We should show our devotion to our faith by having clothes specifically for the use in ritual and should abstain from wearing them for anything else in our lives; however, at the risk of playing devil's advocate ask yourself this: do we really need to dress in robes or the style of clothes that our ancestors wore? Does it make us more of a Heathen than others who don't? Should we get with the times and use our own modern day clothes? Regardless of which way you fall on this discussion we mustn't lose sight of the fact that our ancestors wore those clothes because they were their everyday clothes and they didn't have much of a choice regarding their wardrobe selection! Although the richer you were the more access you had to a far wider choice of textiles, thus giving you more of a choice and also the option to own ritual-specific clothing. However, I believe this was more to do with showing off their wealth and social status rather than any reverence to the Gods and Goddesses. Then again if we wear said clothes does it give us a tangible link to our ancestors and does it make the ritual more responsive due to the fact we are connecting on a deeper level, or is it merely an aesthetic used for our own pleasure? I personally think that we should have the best of both worlds. I myself use a special cloak either worn over my normal clothes or just on its own. I do not dress fully in period costume as I feel it is not necessary and turns my faith into some sort of living history exercise although I do have era-specific items with me when performing ritual. However, I must add and explain my reasoning. I like living history but feel that the religious side is to be kept separate due to the spiritual and emotional concentration needed when performing ritual or magical workings, but this is just my personal opinion.

To Heathen elitists anything less than regimental rituals held with military precision and gatherings organised to the last second amounts to little more than treason within the Heathen community and this is one thing that infuriates me. I am a firm believer that even if you don't partake in all rituals or for that matter any at all it does not make you any less of a Heathen than those who walk around strutting in their period attire whilst reciting the Nine Noble Virtues backwards! As long as you hold the core values, live by the Nine Noble Virtues in your everyday life and conduct yourself with honour and honesty, then as far as I am concerned you are a Heathen Warrior and are of equal standing to those who suggest you are below them! The Gods don't expect you to pray or talk to them every day; they don't expect you to know their whole history and be able to recite it in Old Norse or Anglo-Saxon! It is your choice how much you learn and how far you wish to take your studies. Even if your contribution amounts to little more than a quick "Hail!" looking to the sky whilst walking the dog or a quick "Hail!" followed by the offering of some food and mead for them when feasting, the Gods and Goddesses know your intent. They can see if you are genuine or whether you are just doing it to impress and trying to win favour! Above all else when it concerns rituals, don't be fooled or brainwashed into thinking that you have to do everything someone else does to be a true Heathen. It doesn't work like that. I have often said that our faith is not a religion as such and it should never dominate your life, but enrich it. It should be looked upon as a "morally focused folkish way of life devoid of religious piety but reinforced with courage, underpinned with a social conscience." It is something you carry with you every second of everyday; it is your actions, thoughts and feelings that denote your true sense of being within the Heathen community. Your spiritual and magical essence is forever entwined within our ancestral beliefs. Never doubt they are watching you and never forget that as long as you stay true and don't twist the ideology to suit your own ends the Gods and Goddesses will stand by you and believe in you the way you believe in them. Remember it is a symbiotic relationship; they need us as much as we need them. They need us as their warriors when Ragnarok (the Norse end of days when the forces of good and evil fight and the world begins afresh) happens and we need them for emotional, spiritual and physical growth. Without us believing in them they cease to have any power and will eventually vanish into the realm of myths and legend. Without their support and guidance, along with their belief in us we will never have the ability or gracious humility to grow and evolve into the best man or woman we can be.

Chapter Twelve

Where Do We Go from Here then Clever Clogs?

"The Future awaits the wise guest has his way of dealing

With those who taunt him at table:

He smiles through the meal,

not seeming to hear

The twaddle talked by his foes".

The Havamal

So here we are then, folks! The last chapter. Before we get stuck in, I want you to partake in a little experiment and help me with a burning desire to achieve something completely worthwhile. Don't worry, it isn't anything too drastic and it won't leave you with any lasting damage. (At least I hope not!)

Firstly I want you to close your eyes and relax. Clear everything from your mind and just relax. Count to ten and slowly open your eyes then smile. Yes that's right; I want you to give the biggest smile you have ever given. Think of something that makes you feel happy if it helps. Even if you are a miserable old sausage who hates to show your feelings, do it anyway! I dare say you are feeling more than a little confused and wondering what I'm up to, but rest assured all shall become clear later on.

Over the course of this book we have taken a twisting journey of discovery together. We have explored what it means to follow the Warrior path within the Heathen traditions. We have travelled hundreds of years into the past to try and get the perspective of our ancestors and then scrutinized modern social trends in an attempt to pigeonhole the essence of our heroic culture and how it can help us in today's materialistic world. It has been no easy task; for the soul of our belief structure is as deep as the ocean and before getting to the truth we have to battle our way through a sea of misconceptions and biased rhetoric before reaching the truths we seek. Along the way you may have disagreed with some of the things I have said or might still be a bit confused regarding some of the topics, but don't worry. If you don't agree with some of my views, that is a good thing. To agree and place all your faith blindly in one person's opinion is folly and free thought should always be encouraged. I urge you to investigate yourself, get involved, research and formulate your own theories and explore our faith in your own way. As I said from the outset I don't profess to be an expert and I don't have all the answers and I am still learning and evolving myself; but life has taught me that we have to stand our ground and let people know our thoughts regardless of the reaction. I know in my heart of hearts that I am a good person and that those around me are of the same disposition and share the same values and ethics as I do. I have no time for bullies, racists, bigots and those who lack the strength of character to fight tyranny and evil when they see it and those who blindly follow another without asking questions and investigating themselves. There are many examples I could give regarding actions in my own life that could be seen as "heroic" but these are very personal and even though I have been brutally honest in this book this is not the place to share such intimate knowledge. The bottom line is that we all have that inner strength within us; we all have the capacity for great and noble deeds. All we have to do is have the courage to listen to what our spiritual souls are telling us, harness our magical, physical and emotional energy and realise that our inner warrior soul won't see us wrong. It is the everyday people like you and me who have the capacity to end up doing extraordinary things. I'm not just referring to extreme scenarios like saving someone's life or rescuing someone from a burning building, but rather the little things that some of us take for granted and that ordinarily may be over looked. Any battle, no matter how small or what shape it takes form is a test of our personal resolve and spiritual mindset. It's amazing what we as humans can accomplish if only we listen and learn from the mistakes of the past and resolve ourselves to not making them again. We all know life is full of challenges that can affect us in different ways; it's how we face these trials that separate us from the rest of the populace and shows our true self in the face of adversity.

My aim with this book was threefold, firstly to dispel some of the untruths floating around out there regarding my faith and specifically the warrior path, and secondly to show people that we truly need the primal energy within us and that it can be used for good and as a tool to help our faith grow and evolve. It isn't a negative force as others believe it to be. I'm not going to lie regarding the third reason. It has been a labour of love and has been both enjoyable and infuriating in equal measure but with all honesty, I wouldn't have changed it for the world. I have laid myself bare and open to others who I have no knowledge of and I sincerely hope that I have done my part for the warrior's path. I truly hope that by writing this book I have given at least one reader the inspiration to walk the warrior's path or at least look at the warrior path in a different light. If I have attained this then I feel truly honoured. It's not a case of me being egotistical but rather the fact I whole-heartedly believe in my faith and that I want to play a part in showing the world the REAL morals and ethics that lay the foundations of our folkish religion. When writing I have always tried to remain unbiased and honest in my theories and evaluations. If I have offended you it was not my intention and I apologise. However, there are certain people and groups I won't apologise to and Ragnarok would have been and gone before there was a chance of any apology! These are those people who have warped my faith and moulded it into a twisted ideology of hate and those who believe our faith to be only for the "elite". It is a folk religion, thus meaning for everyone within the folk collective, not just for the select few or those within some secret order. I stand tall and say with a loud voice that I do not agree with you and like I said before think there is no place for you in the Heathen faith. I hope I have made my opinion clear once again, but of course there will be those who don't understand my words and will still tarnish me with the same foul-smelling brush of those I despise and would rather listen to propaganda than investigate themselves. I am fully aware that a possible back lash may happen and that I may receive death threats from some top secret elitist Heathen groups, but if you are one of these people reading this now, remember this: I don't back down and have the courage of my convictions.

So where do we go from here? I and many Heathens that I am in contact with are of the opinion that anyone and everyone with even a slight interest in our folkish belief system should play a part, no matter how small and insignificant it seems in building and restoring our religion and the warrior path. If we all do a little then the overall effect will be magnified; like they say many hands make light work! Any skill you have is useful. If you're an artist, writer, poet or film maker, use your artist skills to explore and promote the true aspects of our faith and bring it to the attention of your friends and those you know. Don't be afraid of ridicule and stay true to your inner feelings. Of course there will be those who dismiss you as some sort of crazy person but don't be downhearted. The Gods respect your efforts and will watch over you. Explore every avenue of our faith and see where your attention gets drawn to, some of you may feel the warrior path is not for you and feel that the magical side presents the biggest challenge and scope for adventure. Follow the path that feels right. Regardless of what you learn and how long it takes you, remember that it is here for you to enjoy and to help enrich your life and those closest to you. Don't be swayed by others' opinions and always remain true to yourself. Formulate your own rituals and give thanks to the Gods and Goddesses in your own way. Like I said before, they know if you are of true intent. We must always be aware that our ancestors lived and breathed this faith twenty-four/seven and it wasn't just something they wheeled out on a Sunday to give the impression of a devotee! Our everyday actions and deeds show the world our moral compass and our ethical resolve. If we falter in any way we not only let ourselves down but our family, kin and faith too. That being said, we will all make mistakes and drop a clanger at some point. We shouldn't be too hard on ourselves because we already know that making mistakes helps us to grow and become better Heathens. Don't you just love religious contradictions!

Discuss with your friends the points raised in this book and see what their reaction is. Some may be intrigued, others not so much. Some may even surprise you to the point of admitting they too have leanings to the warrior path and wish to explore further. Expand your research regarding the warrior path; maybe even write your own book! I really do believe that we must reconnect with our primitive energy and relearn the skills to utilise its immense power. We must arm ourselves with not only the skills to defend and protect those we love but with the knowledge and spiritual mind-set our ancestors possessed. We as a folk people should get out and explore the wonders of the natural world, become one with nature and the majestic flow of divine power that flows through every living thing. We as a species have become arrogant, secure and surrounded by a wealth of technology, using our science as a crutch for those without spiritual fortitude. I truly believe that this disconnection with the Ond energy will be our undoing and we as Heathen Warriors must be of sound mind and of one voice when educating those who have forgotten the real meaning of folk and kin. Not only are we proud Warriors but we are morally balanced and socially aware members of the worldwide community of humans and as such have an ethical responsibility to help others even if they are not of our kin. At this point I feel it is safe to assume that you the reader have a firmer grip on what being a Heathen Warrior is all about and the benefits it has when going about our daily lives. It doesn't mean we have to run around dressed in period clothes, aimlessly waving around a sword or imposing our will on those weaker than us. It doesn't stand for religious dominance and the berating of others of a different faith. It is for all intents and purposes a way of conducting ourselves with honour and listening to our moral compass whilst treating those around us with respect and humility. If these ideals resonate with your inner being then I'm proud to say you are a Heathen Warrior and someone I would be happy to be associated with. You should be proud of the fact that you have the ability to make our ancestors stand up and take notice. Being a Heathen Warrior is not about violence. It is about having the ability to control it so we don't have to subject ourselves or those we love to its destructive force. We, like most of the world, desire peace and freedom above all else. Just because we are prepared to fight for it if we are left with no choice does not make us immoral or less spiritually enlightened than those of other faiths. If you are still of the opinion that we are nothing but mindless thugs just remember one thing, "Sometimes the greatest light comes from the darkest place". Some day you may be glad that we have the skills to protect and defend.

If after reading this you wish to join a group, or for that matter start your own I wish you the best of luck. Feel free to drop me a mail via my publishers to let me know how you're getting on. What I do advise though is that you research any groups or associations thoroughly so that you don't fall in with those of a dubious nature. Make sure they are what they say they are and don't let yourself be fooled by flashy websites and religious spin. Of course you don't have to join a group. You can walk the path alone if you choose, and there are no rules that say you can't. As long as you are living by the Nine Noble Virtues or at least the "meanings" and "actions" behind the words then the Gods and Goddesses are happy to have you on board.

With that said and done it is time for me to bid you a fond farewell and to wish you luck walking your chosen path. Stand tall and do our ancestors proud because I truly believe that they are watching us just like the Gods and Goddesses are, willing us to succeed, and are smiling, content in the fact that our faith has honest and honourable folk forging forward into an uncertain future.

Now I know you are dying to find out what exactly I was talking about when I started this chapter and now the suspense is over....

Even if you haven't enjoyed this book, at least I made you smile.........

In service of the High Ones,

Stuart R Brogan

"Hail to the speaker,

Hail to the knower,

Joy to him who has understood,

Delight to those who have listened."

The Havamal

Lightning Source UK Ltd.
Milton Keynes UK
UKOW01f2101300617
304380UK00009B/388/P